Steve Jobs

LIFE BY DESIGN

Steve Jobs

LIFE BY DESIGN

LESSONS FROM A VISIONARY

GEORGE BEAHM

JAICO PUBLISHING HOUSE

Ahmedabad Bangalore Chennai
Delhi Hyderabad Kolkata Mumbai

Published by Jaico Publishing House
A-2 Jash Chambers, 7-A Sir Phirozshah Mehta Road
Fort, Mumbai - 400 001
jaicopub@jaicobooks.com
www.jaicobooks.com

Published in arrangement with
Hardie Grant Books Ltd
Building 1, 658 Church Street,
Richmond, Victoria 3121
Australia

To be sold only in India, Bangladesh, Bhutan,
Pakistan, Nepal, Sri Lanka and the Maldives.

STEVE JOBS: LIFE BY DESIGN
ISBN 978-81-8495-804-1

First Jaico Impression: 2016
Ninth Jaico Impression: 2023

Printed by
Repro India Limited, Mumbai

Apple, at the core, its core value, believes that people with passion can change the world for the better.

—Steve Jobs

Think different.

—Apple ad

To Mary,

tibi magno cum amor

Contents

Acknowledgements

A BOOK IS A TEAM EFFORT, AND THESE ARE THE people who helped me get the ball to the end zone: my literary agent, Scott Mendel, who challenged me to write another book on Steve Jobs; my wife, Mary, who was my sounding board on this project; and at Palgrave Macmillan, my editor, Karen Wolny; her editorial assistant, Lauren LoPinto, who kept the ball in motion; Alan Bradshaw, production, who shepherded the book; Abimbola Oladipo, production assistant; and Rachel Lodi in the publicity department.

I am especially grateful to the eagle-eyed Debra Manette, who copyedited the manuscript, and measurably improved it.

Thank you, all.

INTRODUCTION

Steve Jobs' Three Stories

Jobs was not a rousing orator. He looked nervous as he approached the podium. As he spoke, though, his voice gained the strength of someone who knows that what he's saying is both true and very important. And something unusual happened: we all started paying attention.

We still are.

—Sheena Chestnut Greitens, Stanford class of 2005

BAREFOOT HIPPIE TURNED BILLIONAIRE

AN ESTIMATED 23,000 PEOPLE PACKED THE stadium on 11 June 2005 for Stanford University's 114th commencement.

The unconventional keynote speaker, dressed in the traditional black robe and cardinal-colour hood, wore sandals and blue jeans underneath.

He graduated from high school with mostly Cs and Bs and a cumulative grade-point average of 2.65. He dropped out of college after six months. He came of age in 1975, just as the Vietnam War ended. He rejected Christianity to embrace Zen Buddhism. He neither chased money for its own sake nor sought fame – but both came to him in large measure.

This barefoot hippie became a multibillionaire, a highly respected CEO, and one of the most famous people on the planet. He was especially admired by young people who considered him to be an inspirational figure, a rock star in his own right. It was his success, especially his comeback act at the company he co-founded, that earned him the privilege of sharing his life's lessons with Stanford's graduating class.

President John Hennessy warmly welcomed the assemblage. He was followed by Provost John Etchemendy for the presentation of awards. Then Hennessy returned to the podium to introduce the beaming fifty-year-old man with a sheaf of papers and an iPhone in hand.

Though the keynote speaker was never formally a student at Stanford, it was a second home to him. He enjoyed walking around its beautiful campus. He'd spoken to its Graduate School of Business, where he always found a ready audience. He'd also had surgery to remove part of his pancreas at the university's medical centre. And Stanford's burgeoning Apple Computer collections held hundreds of boxes of documents from his company that formed a nucleus supplemented by artefacts, documents and memorabilia from other sources.

The commencement speaker's prepared text ran exactly 2,250 words, which he delivered in twenty-two minutes. It covered three major themes – life, love and death – corresponding to the beginning, middle and the end of his life.

He deliberately used the storytelling mode, because people listen to stories; he wanted to make sure they listened. Lectures and speeches? Not his style. He always preferred to engage the audience.

The famous figure was Steve Jobs, and the stories he told – all the more powerful because of their simplicity – struck a responsive chord with the audience and reverberated worldwide.

After Stanford posted it online, in video and print form, Jobs' address went viral. The streaming video went on to become the most watched commencement address in history with 26 million viewers worldwide.[1]

The commencement address itself – intuitive, simple and direct – was pure Steve Jobs. He solicited feedback from his wife, Laurene, but otherwise wrote it himself. Spun gold, it is a web of words that holds our attention and captivates our minds. All the world's a stage, but he was a player who commanded attention: Nobody could do it better.

A man who zealously guarded his privacy, who rarely talked about personal matters in public, Steve Jobs spoke from the heart and, in the process, left an indelible impression on our own hearts.

He did what he does best – he simplified … and delivered an insanely great commencement address. Infamous for his 'reality distortion field',[2] Jobs did not need to employ it on that day. He simply told of life's joys and sorrows, and that was enough.

Jobs' address can be taken as his 'last lecture'. As the late Randy Pausch wrote, the last lecture

> has become a common exercise on college campuses. Professors are asked to consider their demise and to ruminate on what matters most to them. And while they speak, audiences can't help but mull the same question: What wisdom would we impart to the world if we knew it was our

> last chance? If we had to vanish tomorrow, what would we want as our legacy?[3]

Jobs, who knew he was living on borrowed time, had surely been asked to give commencement addresses over the course of his career,[4] but this was the only one he gave.

Six short years after Jobs gave that commencement address, he died.

He was fifty-six years old.

~

In *Steve Jobs*, biographer Walter Isaacson compared Jobs to inventors Edison and Ford. Those are fair comparisons, but Jobs was principally a visionary; thus, Jobs is similar to Walt Disney in that respect. Disney pioneered Imagineering, the art of combining imagination with engineering; he created the first full-length animated films, and amazed us all; and he gave us unforgettable consumer experiences at his theme parks around the world – characteristics Jobs also encompassed.

It's a small world, after all, and in retrospect, it seems fitting that the Walt Disney Company, the distributor of Pixar's movies, would later consolidate operations and buy the company outright.

In a perfect world, Jobs would have lived well into his late eighties. He would have become the elder statesman in the information technology field, like his longtime frenemy Bill

Gates. He would have retired when he had accomplished all he wanted to do and sailed around the world on the yacht he designed, *Venus.* He would have lived long enough to see his custom-designed, Japanese-influenced home built. He would have been able to watch his kids grow into adulthood and play with his grandchildren; and he would have been able to share the rest of his long life with his wife, Laurene Powell, whom he loved beyond all telling.

We all die, as Jobs' sister Mona Simpson said in her eulogy for him, *in media res* – in the middle of things. The nature of life is always unfinished business.

Steve Jobs was sanguine about his medical condition, but it was a battle he didn't win, though not for lack of trying. He never gave up the good fight; he raged against the dying of the light. He celebrated life and took from each day small and large measures of happiness, which gave him the strength to carry on.

He was determined to live long enough to see his son Reed graduate from high school, and he did. As Mona Simpson told us in her eulogy, everyone who was at the graduation party afterward would always remember the sight of the two dancing together – a proud son and an even prouder father.

THE GENIUS OF JOBS

What made Jobs' accomplishments all the more remarkable was that he didn't tread the traditional path to success by being trained in a specific discipline. He also didn't take the path less travelled. What he did was clear a path through the jungle so the rest of us could follow.

He was not an engineer, a programmer or an artist, nor did he have an MBA. Instead he drew inspiration from all those disciplines – technology and the liberal arts – and saw the world differently. He had a clearly defined goal fuelled by passion and persistence, and the products of his febrile imagination left us all amazed.

That was Steve Jobs' genius.

Like Jobs, we all may not necessarily have the specific talents to design the mechanical components of a product, program a computer by writing code, draw art, or master the complexities of business sufficient to earn an advanced degree. But we can take our innate talents – whatever they are – and, fuelled by passion and persistence with a specific goal in mind, we too can make our dreams come true. He inspires us to climb higher.

That is Jobs' legacy.

~

January 2014 marked thirty years since the first Mac computer made its debut. How wonderful it would have been for Steve Jobs to have stuck around to attend Apple's birthday party and blow out the candles on the cake, celebrating a seminal computer that he knew would change the world.

'Apple's core strength is to bring very high technology to mere mortals in a way that surprises and delights them and that they can figure out how to use,' Jobs once said.[5]

That speaks to the very heart of the Macintosh.

Apple proudly posted on its home page in January 2014:

> In 1984, Apple introduced the world to Macintosh ... And it came with a promise – that the power of technology ... could change the world. That promise has been kept. Today we create, connect, share, and learn in ways that were unimaginable 30 years ago. Imagine what we can accomplish in the next 30 years.[6]

Jobs' greatest invention was not the Mac or any of his other innovative products but, as he frequently said, Apple itself. We are reminded of what Walt Disney said:

> Well, my greatest reward I think is ... I've been able to build this wonderful organisation ... I feel I can ... have the public appreciate and accept what I've done all these years. That is a great reward.[7]

Toward that end, Jobs put in place a succession plan to ensure the continuity of the company well into the future. He hand-trained a management team to carry on the company's mission – to create great consumer products that would empower people and change their lives.

Steve Jobs reluctantly stepped down when it was clear that he no longer had a choice. It was one of the most painful but necessary decisions of his life. Although he had been forced from his own company twice – the first time in a power play and the second time due to illness – this time around, he quarterbacked the play: He ensured that his chief operating officer, Tim Cook, was ready to take over so that Apple never missed a beat.

And the beat goes on.

~

Jobs revolutionised several industries, any one of which would have been enough for a lifelong career. But that was not his style. He rocketed through life because he knew time was always short; he frequently said that he wanted to 'make a dent in the universe' and designed his life accordingly; in doing so, he changed our world.

Note to the Reader

THIS BOOK IS NOT MEANT TO BE A SUBSTITUTE for viewing or reading Jobs' commencement address. I strongly urge you to view his address before reading this book, which quotes him and summarises his own words, draws on stories from his life and also connects some dots. In short, this book builds on what Steve Jobs said in his address and sheds light on its explicit and implicit themes.

Steve Jobs' commencement address is available on the World Wide Web in text and video from Stanford University at:

http://news.stanford.edu/news/2005/june15/jobs-061505.html

Regarding the quotations that open each chapter, they are drawn from Jobs' commencement address, unless noted otherwise.

FIRST STORY

Connecting the Dots

JOBS OBSERVED THAT LIFE'S GRAND DESIGN, THE pattern of life, can be discerned by looking back with the perspective that only time can provide.

1

Great Expectations

'I decided to drop out.'

1

MR JANDALI'S SON

EVEN BEFORE STEVE JOBS WAS BORN, HIS BIOlogical parents had high educational aspirations for him, and no wonder: Abdulfattah 'John' Jandali's own father placed a premium on education. It is not surprising then that John Jandali went on to earn his PhD at the University of Wisconsin. Jobs' biological mother, Joanne Schieble, a graduate student in speech therapy, also placed a premium on education.[1] But because her father objected to her dating, much less marrying, a Syrian man, she put her unborn child up for adoption, with a proviso: The adopting parents had to be college graduates.

In a twist of fate, the college graduates who were set to adopt Jandali and Schieble's child had their hearts set on a girl, so when Schieble gave birth to a boy, they declined to adopt. The boy then went to the next couple on the waiting list, Paul and Clara Jobs, presumed by Schieble to be college graduates. When Schieble found out that both had dropped out of high school, she extracted a promise from them: Her son would have to go to college. Paul and Clara Jobs reluctantly agreed, but that eventual promise would prove to be an economic hardship for the blue-collar family who wanted to adopt a child.

Born on 24 February 1955, the child was named Steven Paul Jobs.

COLLEGE BOUND

Growing up in Los Altos, south of San Francisco, Steve Jobs had no lack of colleges to choose from, including nearby Stanford University. Stanford justifiably enjoys legendary status in Silicon Valley's history because of its pioneering role in computer breakthroughs: Internet protocols (TCP/IP) were developed by Professor Vinton Cerf; two alumni, Jerry Yang and David Filo, founded Yahoo!; and two graduate students, Sergey Brin and Larry Page, developed the groundbreaking page-rank algorithms for an early version of Google. Stanford cited other key Silicon Valley companies with a strong connection to the university, including Cisco Systems, Intuit, Silicon Graphics, and Sun Microsystems.[2]

Stanford also counted among its alumni the founders of Hewlett-Packard, whose suburban garage is, according to the university's website, 'the Birthplace of Silicon Valley'. A little-known fact is that Steve Jobs, when he was twelve, had an early encounter with Bill Hewlett of Hewlett-Packard:

> When he was in eighth grade, Steve Jobs decided to build a frequency counter for a school project and needed parts.

> Someone suggested that he call Bill Hewlett. Finding a William Hewlett in the telephone book, the 12-year-old Jobs called and asked, 'Is this the Bill Hewlett of Hewlett-Packard?'
>
> 'Yes,' said Bill. Jobs made his request. Bill spent some time talking to him about his project.
>
> Several days later, Jobs went to HP and picked up a bag full of parts that Bill had put together for him.[3]

Subsequently, Jobs landed a summer job at HP between his freshman and sophomore years at Homestead High.

On the face of it, Stanford University might have been a good fit for Jobs, but as he later explained: 'I wanted something that was more artistic and interesting.'[4]

Moreover, Stanford was an expensive school and would have strained the budget of Jobs' adoptive parents. The educational alternative was a state-supported California college with lower tuition fees. But California schools held no interest for Jobs. Instead, after a visit to Reed College in Portland, Oregon, he set his mind to enrol there. His adoptive parents had learned early on that their smart but stubborn son was the classic immovable object. Recognising a lost cause, his parents surrendered to the inevitable and braced themselves for the expense of out-of-state college tuition, room and board.

The promise Paul and Clara Jobs made to Joanne Schieble, their son's biological mother, would be realised: Her son would go to college – regardless of the cost.[5]

REED COLLEGE

There was, as Steve Jobs found out, a big difference between how he viewed his role as a student at Reed College and the college's expectations of him. Jobs put a lot of emphasis on the 'liberal' and the 'arts' of Reed College, but the college placed its emphasis on its demanding curriculum. According to the college web page: 'Reed provides one of the nation's most intellectually rigorous undergraduate experiences, with a highly structured program balancing broad distribution requirements and in-depth study in a chosen academic discipline.'[6]

That wasn't what Steve Jobs expected. 'They are making me take all these courses,' he complained to his friend Steve 'Woz' Wozniak, an electronics wizard whom Jobs had met through a mutual friend, Bill Fernandez, when he was in high school. To which Woz replied nonchalantly, 'Yes, that's what they do in college.'[7]

Jobs' unrealistic expectations of college – as a place to meet girls and learn whatever he wanted on his own terms – were shattered when reality set in. After six frustrating months of marching to the beat of the same drummer as his fellow freshmen, Jobs realised he was out of step with them. Living a bohemian lifestyle, he bristled at the academic constraints. Clearly, the path Jobs' adoptive parents had agreed to with his birth mother was not the one he wanted to follow.

A college degree is widely considered to be a necessary ticket to success, but according to Jeremy Kahn in a *Fortune* magazine article, 'for many people, the value of a college education is in friendships made (or forgone) and new roads taken (or not). In this sense, the economic arguments may miss the point.' Parents, Kahn explained, 'want to know whether it's worth it for their little darling. And that's a question economists can't answer.'[8]

In Jobs' case, the point was moot because he would eventually drop out permanently from Reed College,[9] rejecting formal education in favour of informal education, recalling Mark Twain's wry comment: 'I have never let my schooling interfere with my education.' For Jobs, observation and experience – life itself – would be his teachers.

~

Have the courage to live your life, not the one imagined for you by well-intentioned parents or other authority figures. You will know what's best.

2

Seize the Day

'Your time is limited.'

'TIME IS ON MY SIDE,' CROONED THE Rolling Stones, but it's not a sentiment Steve Jobs shared. At an early age, Jobs was acutely aware of life's fleeting nature: Unlike money, of which he had plenty later in life, time could not be replaced.

Therefore, it was no surprise that Jobs believed in the philosophy inherent in *carpe diem*, or 'seize the day'. It means living life to its fullest every day. The phrase comes from the *Odes* by Horace, a Latin poet.

Jobs' first girlfriend, Chrisann Brennan, explained that 'Steve always believed he was going to die young. I think that's part of what gave his life such urgency. He never expected to live past 45.'[1]

THE DAYS OF YOUR LIFE

Bruce J. Klein, director of the nonprofit Immortality Institute, wrote that 'with few exceptions, 30,000 days is the average human lifespan – 40,000 if you're lucky'.[2]

Steve Jobs wasn't so lucky. He lived only 20,984 days.

But when Jobs died, he was at the top of his game, and he squeezed time like a fruit to extract every sweet drop.

Impatient by nature and inclination, Jobs chafed at schedules set by others for him. For instance, after enrolling at Reed College and realising the administration had radically different ideas on what direction his education should take, Jobs simply stopped taking the scheduled classes. Instead, he audited classes of interest. He strongly felt that academia existed to serve him, and not vice versa.

JOBS' JOBS

Twenty-nine years old when he was interviewed by *Playboy* magazine, Jobs was, at that time, the youngest person on the *Forbes* list of richest Americans, with a net worth (mostly in Apple Computer stock) estimated at $450 million.[3]

In May 1985, three months after the *Playboy* interview hit the newsstands, Jobs was relieved of his duties as the head of the Macintosh division, after losing a power struggle with his mentor, John Sculley, and started a computer company called NeXT. He also bought a computer division, later renamed Pixar, from filmmaker George Lucas. Jobs took Pixar public soon after the first *Toy Story* movie was released, then eventually sold the company to Disney and became a paper billionaire, based on stock valuation.

Riding high on his success with Pixar, in 1997 Jobs was the proverbial comeback kid when he was wooed by Gil Amelio, who was then Apple's chief executive officer (CEO). Jobs returned as interim CEO but soon took the job permanently. In his second act at Apple, Jobs kick started a demoralised company that had fundamentally lost its way. It was Jobs' subsequent products – iTunes, the iPod, iPhone, and iPad – that saved Apple from becoming pulped.

~

Until the end of his days, Jobs believed in seizing the day. Masayoshi Son, CEO of a Japanese telecommunications company called Softbank, recounted a telling anecdote. Son said that he was in a meeting with Jobs' successor, Apple CEO Tim Cook, who was forced to cut it short when he was called to duty. According to Son, Cook apologised and said that 'Steve is calling me because he wants to talk about [our] next product.'[4] Cook left the meeting to go straight to Jobs' house.

That was the day before Jobs died.

No one would have expected Jobs, at that point in his life, to concern himself with business matters. But he did so because it was important to him.

He seized the day. He *lived* every day as if it were his last.

~

Jobs' life philosophy was, in the words of James Dean, 'Dream as if you will live forever; live as if you will die today.'

By living that philosophy to the max, Jobs simply accomplished more. He revolutionised not only one business but several, as musician Bono pointed out. 'He changed music. He changed film. He changed the personal computer. It's a wonderful encouragement to people who want to think differently, that's where artists connect with him.'[5]

Jobs' industriousness stemmed from a saying he first encountered as a teenager. Though restated by many people over the years, the original dates back to Marcus Aurelius, a Roman emperor who wrote that one should 'live each day as if it were thy last – without haste, or pause, or sloth, or hypocrisy'.[6]

Steve Jobs did just that.

Each day is a treasure, so treasure each day.

3

Cultivate Your Curiosity

'... my curiosity and intuition turned out to be priceless later on.'

TWO JAPANESE LANDMARKS – MOUNT FUJI and Kyoto's Temple of the Dragon at Peace, a Zen garden at Ryōan-ji – can be found among the desktop images in Maverick, the current Mac operating system.

As with all things Apple, their inclusion is deliberate.

Though Jobs never climbed Mount Fuji, he loved walking among the rock gardens in Kyoto, which he visited on a regular basis, often in the company of his children, who knew it was one of his favourite places.

What's little known is that Jobs' curiosity regarding Japanese culture was instrumental in helping to shape and reinforce his business philosophies. His interest was also reflected in the products themselves – simple, elegant, small and beautiful.

~

In his Stanford address, Jobs tells an oft-repeated story about how his casual interest in calligraphy, which was a result of a chance encounter at Reed College, led to the Macintosh's fonts. It's a great story, but so well known that Stanford graduates likely knew it already. For that reason, it's more instructive to look at one of his other interests that, over the years, grew to become important – Japan.

Innately curious about Japanese culture and business, Jobs incorporated Nippon values into his own life, personally and professionally. A detailed discussion is beyond the scope of this book, but hitting the high points provides food for thought: Just as Jobs straddled technology and the liberal arts, he comfortably straddled Eastern and Western culture, Japanese and American.

Food: A vegetarian in college and, later, a pescetarian, Jobs loved fresh sushi (especially eel) and soba (noodles).

Sushi, which is a visual and gastronomic treat, requires the freshest seafood, finest rice and special vinegar to make each bite a savoury delight.

Similarly, soba, made from buckwheat flour, is prepared on the spot and is served hot or cold; hot with a broth, cold with a dipping sauce.

It stands to reason that while in Japan, Jobs took full advantage of the local cuisine because of its authenticity and great taste.

Back home, Jobs frequented two Palo Alto restaurants – Jinsho and Kaygetsu – where the food was carefully prepared by experienced Japanese chefs. (When Kaygetsu closed, Jobs wooed its chef to Apple's cafeteria, to the delight of its employees who shared Jobs' enthusiasm for authentic Japanese cuisine.)

Clothing: During a business trip to Japan in the company of John Sculley, Jobs asked Sony chairman and co-founder Akio Morita why the employees all wore uniforms. Morita explained that after the war, the Japanese people had very little to wear. Companies provided uniforms so workers would not feel ashamed; they'd have presentable clothes to wear to work.

That led Jobs to commission a uniform for Apple employees, a jacket designed by Issey Miyake. American employees, though, bristled and voiced their opposition to wearing any uniform, and Jobs permanently retired that idea. For himself, he commissioned Miyake to design a turtleneck shirt; worn with pressed Levi's jeans without a belt and New Balance sneakers, it became his trademark look, which is what he wore most of the time, on and off work.

Miyake made one hundred shirts for Jobs, filling his closet. Zen-like in its simplicity, Jobs' simple wardrobe was functional and distinctive.

Japanese craftsmanship: In the mid-1990s, Steve Jobs and his wife went to a Kyoto gallery where they saw the work of a porcelain artist named Yukio Shakunaga. Jobs made three trips to the one-week show, and bought several pieces.[1]

Though he didn't speak Japanese, and Shakunaga's English was broken, they conversed using pen and paper. Jobs was curious about the white clay called *hakudo* that the artist exclusively used; he dug it out of the ground himself, unlike other porcelain artists who were content to simply buy their clay.

Jobs ordered more pieces for his collection when he returned to California.

Jobs' fascination with Shakunaga's manufacturing process recalls a comment former Apple CEO John Sculley made about Jobs: 'He was a person of huge vision. But he was also a person that believed in the precise detail of every step. He was methodical and careful about everything – a perfectionist to the end.'[2]

SOUND BUSINESS PRACTICES

Jobs' inquisitiveness also led him to innovate his business. He studied Akio Morita's career to see how he could improve Apple's products. As Jobs was fond of saying (a comment attributed to Pablo Picasso), good artists copy but great artists steal. During their 1985 trip to Japan, John Sculley and Jobs toured Sony's high-tech factories that inspired the Macintosh factories. Recalls Sculley, 'Steve's point of reference was Sony at the time. He really wanted to be Sony. He didn't want to be IBM. He didn't want to be Microsoft. He wanted to be Sony.' Sculley elaborated:

> We used to go visit Akio Morita and he had really the same kind of high-end standards that Steve did and respect for beautiful products. I remember Akio Morita gave Steve and me each one of the first Sony Walkmans. None of us had

> ever seen anything like that before because there had never been a product like that. This is 25 years ago and Steve was fascinated by it. The first thing he did with his was take it apart and he looked at every single part. How the fit and finish was done, how it was built.[3]

Jobs' curiosity also extended to the Japanese way of business, which recognises that because the customer is king, the customer experience is of paramount importance. Morita explains the Japanese way of taking care of the customer in his autobiography, *Made in Japan:*

> [B]ecause Japan's consumers are fussy, we cannot sell anything that is not of high quality. After-sales service is crucial; we will still make house calls, and the company that lets up on any aspect of production or delivery or service will lose customers. An American in the cosmetics business was shocked to hear that it is not unusual for a wholesaler in Japan to send a single lipstick by messenger all the way across the city to a retailer with a waiting customer. If he didn't, it was explained, he might lose the retail shop's business.[4]

Jobs adopted the Japanese way of doing business and improved on it, taking the best of those philosophies to integrate them into his own.

A careful study of Morita's autobiography also shows Japanese sensibilities that influenced Jobs' thinking and, by extension, Apple's. Clearly, Morita and Jobs were of like minds.

Here are some examples from Morita's book that could just as easily have come from Jobs' playbook.

Creativity:

> It is possible to have a good idea, a fine invention, but still miss the boat, so product planning, which means deciding how to use technology in a given product, demands creativity. And once you have a good product it is important to use creativity in marketing it. Only with these three kinds of creativity – technology, product planning, and marketing – can the public receive the benefit of a new technology.[5]

Apple has always put a premium on infusing creativity in every phase, from inception to product delivery. Apple always hires the best ad agencies – sometimes pitting them against each other, to spur them on – and the company itself is synonymous with creativity.

Winning over the consumer:

> It lies on the shelves and the showroom floors of stores all around the world: good quality products that people want and in such variety that any consumer whim can be satisfied. This is how Japanese goods managed to take so much of the U.S. market. And I would say that the best way to compete with the Japanese would be to examine the successful Japanese products for design and construction and innovative concepts.[6]

Japanese consumers are among the most discriminating in the world. They have come to expect product excellence and demand it, so Japanese manufacturers deliver – or go out of business quickly. To surprise and delight the fickle Japanese public, especially with electronic products, is a formidable challenge.

Apple however seems to have conquered that challenge. The company's products, especially its iPhone, are in big demand in Japan. When the iPhone 5 was announced, one customer got in line at Apple's Ginza store in Tokyo ten days before its release date.

Other Japanese customers who queued up behind him wrapped themselves in rain gear and braved a typhoon that lashed the country.

> Right before the typhoon hit Tokyo, the handful of people lined up were moved into the Apple store to take refuge … There, they were allowed to bring in their wet possessions, rest in the Apple store theatre until 10 a.m., and were even given bottled water.[7]

That experience prompted one long-waiting customer to exclaim, 'I was so moved how Apple treats its customers.'[8]

Future design:

It is frequently said in Japan, quite rightly, that the thrust of Japan industry in the seventies and eighties has been toward things that are light, thin, short and small. We expect that this will hold for the future as well.[9]

Think iPod, iPhone, and iPad. All are good examples of how Jobs constantly fought to improve, simplify and ensure his products had the smallest possible 'footprints'.

Haste makes waste:

> I have been dealing with Americans for many years and they are always in a hurry. It is common to hear in America: 'There's no time!' 'Do it now!' 'He who hesitates is lost!'[10]

Jobs, who never rushed a product to market, had his own timetable. He always invested the necessary amount of time to ensure the product was perfection right down to its smallest component. As Jobs liked to tell Tim Cook, 'Details matter, it's worth waiting to get it right.'[11]

Reinvention:

> Our perhaps peculiarly Japanese reaction when we learn of some new development or come across a phenomenon, is invariably 'How can I use this? What can I make with it? How can it be used to produce a useful product?'[12]

Thomas Edison remarked, 'I'm a good sponge. I absorb ideas and put them to use. Most of my ideas first belonged to people who didn't bother to develop them.'

Like Edison, Steve Jobs was a reinventor who also was quick to recognise and capitalise on good ideas. He was more a reimagineer than he was an imagineer: He looked at the screens of personal computers that displayed only one font and gave us the world's first personal computer with multiple fonts, a mouse and a graphical user interface (GUI). He took the klutzy MP3 player with its limited memory and awkward user interface and transformed it into a sleek, small, intuitively designed iPod music player. He took the clamshell-designed mobile phone with a user-hostile interface and web access using tiny keys and gave us a touch-sensitive screen, a user-friendly operating system, and countless apps that simply worked. He took the stylus-based tablet and gave us the elegant iPad.

~

Jobs borrowed and then improved on Sony's business practices, which were pivotal in making Apple products that appealed to everybody, including Japanese consumers who demand the very best.

~

> ***Cultivating curiosity for its own sake can lead to unexpected results in ways that are unforeseen – life can be delightfully serendipitous.***

4

Think Like an Artist

'If you want to live your life in a creative way, as an artist, you have to not look back too much. You have to be willing to take whatever you've done and whoever you were and throw them away.'

—in *Playboy* magazine, February 1985

4

I CAN'T GET NO SATISFACTION

THE COMPUTER INDUSTRY'S ELEPHANTS' Graveyard is littered with the plastic bodies of obsolete personal computers. Who even remembers, for instance, the Commodore PET or any of its lacklustre brethren? Commodore's story is a minor, if ironic, footnote in computer history: When Apple was a fledgling company, between the release of the Apple I and Apple II, Steve Jobs offered to sell it to Commodore.

Jack Tramiel, then president of Commodore, refused because he 'thought it was ridiculous to spend $100,000 on two guys in a garage'.[1]

Tramiel chose poorly.

Later, after the Apple II proved there was a burgeoning market for personal computers, everyone was jumping on the bandwagon – including Commodore. Its PET computer deliberately undercut Apple II's price by several hundred dollars, but its keyboard was designed for munchkins, and substandard engineering resulted in poor reliability. As Woz remarked, 'They left out expandability, colour, good memory, high-resolution graphics, a nice keyboard, the ability to use your TV ... all sorts of things.'[2] Commodore's PET computer eventually had to be put to sleep.

Twelve years after PET's release, Commodore went down the commode; the company is now defunct.

The pervasive problem in the industry was that manufacturers never set out to create great products. Blinded by the money, they rushed poorly made products to the marketplace and hoped they would sell quickly, dumping them on unsuspecting customers. It was a seduction of the innocent, and it was simply bad business for companies and bad news for duped consumers.

By the early eighties, it was time for someone to think differently about computers. Instead of inexpensive knock-offs, it was time for manufacturers to think about pride, craftsmanship and customer satisfaction. It was time to stop imitating and start innovating because that's what it takes to make as big a dent in the universe as possible. It was about idealism and changing the world. It was about rethinking how people interact with computers, and making them as simple as possible – like household appliances. It was time to design computers for the ordinary person, not the tech heads who enjoyed programming them.

As Mac team member Andy Hertzfeld explained in his book, *Revolution in the Valley: The Insanely Great Story of How the Mac Was Made:*

> A few years earlier, the Apple II and other pioneering systems made computing affordable to individuals, but they were still much too hard for most people to use. We felt that the Mac's graphical user interface had the potential to make computing enjoyable to nontechnical users for the very first time, potentially improving the lives of millions of users.[3]

Enter Steve Jobs.

ARTIST'S SENSIBILITIES

Steve Jobs was not an artist in the traditional sense. He couldn't draw. And unlike his Apple co-founder, Steve Wozniak, Jobs couldn't code or design an elegant circuit board. Jobs was not a musician, a sculptor or a writer. But he clearly was, in its largest sense, an artist: He was creative and could see what others couldn't, and he brought people together to make his dream come true. He thought much like Walt Disney, who explained:

> My role? Well, you know I was stumped one day when a little boy asked, 'Do you draw Mickey Mouse?' I had to admit I do not draw anymore. 'Then you think up all the jokes and ideas?'
>
> 'No,' I said. 'I don't do that.'
>
> Finally, he looked at me and said, 'Mr Disney, just what do you do?'

> 'Well,' I said, 'sometimes I think of myself as a little bee. I go from one area of the studio to another and gather pollen and sort of stimulate everybody. I guess that's the job I do.'[4]

On the Mac project, Jobs' responsibility was to be an impresario who inspired and orchestrated a small group of mostly men in their twenties who, like him, saw themselves as artists. As Jobs recalled:

> The people working on the Macintosh were musicians, artists, poets, zoologists and historians who also happened to be the best computer scientists in the world ... We all brought to this effort a very liberal arts attitude that we wanted to pull in the best we saw in the other fields into this field. I don't think you get that if you're very narrow.[5]

Jobs' band of merry pirates, as he characterised the Mac group, were fired up with passion and creativity and wanted to create something great.

Steve Wozniak, speaking about the Mac team, recalled that 'this cast of young and inexperienced people who cared more than anything about doing great things created what is perhaps the key technology of our lives ... [It was a time when] the rules of innovation were guided by internal rewards, and not by money.'[6]

They were perfectionists and workaholics whose personal relationships suffered because work came first, especially as the work hours s-t-r-e-t-c-h-e-d as the final deadline approached.

They were keenly aware that every aspect of the Mac – from coding to the screen display and the machine itself – required intense focus to get every detail just right. They took great pride in their work, knowing that if they could come together and pull it off, they could change the world, because they knew that one day, all computers would be like Macs.

Mac team member Andy Hertzfeld recalled:

> The Mac team had a complicated set of motivations, but the most unique ingredient was a strong dose of artistic values. First and foremost, Steve Jobs thought of himself as an artist, and he encouraged the design team to think of themselves that way, too. The goal was never to beat the competition or to make a lot of money; it was to do the greatest thing possible, or even a little greater.[7]

AN ARTIST SIGNS HIS WORK

On 10 February 1982, recalled Hertzfeld, the original Mac team gathered around a large piece of drawing paper on a table. 'Steve gave a little speech about artists signing their work, and then cake and champagne were served as he called each team member to step forward and sign their name for posterity.'[8]

Their names were permanently etched on the inside of the Mac's plastic case – not that anyone could see them: Jobs had built the Mac so that a special tool was required simply to open it. In doing so, he sent an unmistakable message: Please leave our work of art alone. Accept it as is. Don't break into it and tinker with it.

The Mac team members' signatures were legible, signed with obvious care, to ensure each name could be read. Among them, two stood out because of their simplicity: 'Woz' and, in lower case, 'steven jobs'.

THE MACINTOSH SPIRIT

In the epilogue to *Revolution in the Valley*, Andy Hertzfeld wrote:

> Most commercial products are driven by commercial values, where the goal is to maximise profits by outperforming your competition. In contrast, the Macintosh was driven more by artistic values, oblivious to competition, where the goal was to be transcendently brilliant and insanely great ...[9]

Jobs celebrated what was called the 'Macintosh spirit', which was only possible in a working environment characterised by, as Mac engineer Andy Hertzfeld put it, 'urgency, ambition, passion for excellence, artistic pride, and irreverent humour'. The Mac team members' shared passion was what made all their sacrifices worthwhile, as they worked toward a common goal. It was, said Hertzfeld, an example to emulate, and one that would be inspirational for decades to come.[10]

~

Think like an artist to create great works of art that people will want to own and that will also stand the test of time.

5

Think Big but Start Small

'Woz and I started Apple in my parents' garage when I was 20.'

AS JOBS TOLD STANFORD'S GRADUATES, APPLE started in a garage in 1976 with just himself and Steve Wozniak,[1] but over the next decade it grew into a $2 billion company with over four thousand employees.

APPLE I

Consider an apple tree: Germinating from a single seed, it can grow into a tree twenty feet high; one seed, one tree, and bushels of apples. Similarly, the Apple Computer germinated from a single seed planted in Steve Jobs' fertile mind. When he saw Wozniak's elegantly designed circuit board, he knew he could sell it to electronic hobbyists, so why not make money by starting their own computer company?

They came up with a company name (Apple Computer) and dubbed the PC board Apple I, which they advertised in *Interface Age*, a computer magazine. The ad tempted hobbyists to 'Byte into an Apple' for $666.66,[2] which at first glance appears to be an arbitrarily arrived at price, but in fact was the result of number-crunching. According to Owen Linzmayer, who has written extensively about Apple Computer for over twenty years,

> Jobs set the list price of the original 4K Apple I at $666.66 by doubling the cost of manufacturing, allowing dealers a 33.3 per cent markup on the wholesale price of $500. Fundamentalist Christians were quick to complain that 666 was the 'mark of the beast'. Jobs blew these people off by explaining he had taken 7 (a so-called mystical number), subtracted 1 (another mystical number), and arrived at a perfectly innocent price.[3]

The headline for the ad in *Interface Age* read: 'Apple Introduces the First Low Cost Microcomputer System with a Video Terminal and 8K Bytes of RAM on a Single PC Card.'

The Apple I was clearly not a computer for the rest of us. It was for hardcore electronic hobbyists only, who'd have to add peripherals to make it truly useful: a power supply, keyboard, case, monitor and cassette tape recorder to run its Apple Basic software.

According to Apple's ad, it was 'a truly complete microcomputer system on a single PC board' and promised to be

> essentially 'hassle free' and you can be running within minutes ... The Apple Computer makes it possible for many people with limited budgets to step up to a video terminal as an I/O [input/output] device for their computer.[4]

Apple's first bulk order for fifty computers from the Byte Shop in Mountain View was an unforeseen financial windfall – $500 per computer, or $25,000. Steve Wozniak recalled that it was 'the biggest single episode in the company's history. Nothing in subsequent years was so great and so unexpected. It was not what we had intended to do.'[5]

Jobs and Wozniak originally had intended to sell a handful to fellow hobbyists at the gathering hole for fellow geeks, the Homebrew Club.

APPLE COMPUTER

Starting a computer company certainly wasn't what Woz had intended to do, but it *was* what Steve Jobs intended to do. However, it would require more than a handful of small orders from local computer stores to go national. Apple would need proper funding and to be properly set up as a business, which happened in November 1976, when former Intel executive Armas 'Mike' Markkula, Jr, came out of retirement to help Apple get on its feet by investing $92,000 of his own money and securing $250,000 in a line of credit from Bank of America.

APPLE II

Apple Computer filed incorporation papers on 3 January 1977, and in the subsequent year, Apple released the Apple II, which sold for $1,298. Unlike the Apple I, the Apple II was more customer-friendly, with an integrated keyboard, case, dual disc drives and a monitor.

The Apple II was the firm foundation on which Apple was built, paying for and paving the way for the Macintosh in 1984.

And it all began in a one-car garage at a ranch-style home in Los Altos, California.

THE HOUSE THAT BUILT APPLE

The house at 2066 Crist Drive in Los Altos, California, was built in 1952, on the site of a former apricot orchard. The house, bought for $21,000 by Paul and Clara Jobs, is the official birthplace of Apple Computer.

Designated by the Los Altos Historical Commission as a 'historic resource', the 1,793-square-foot, three-bedroom ranch-style house is now worth an estimated $1.5 million; its current owner is Steve Jobs' adoptive sister, Patty.

But in 1976 it was Apple Computer headquarters, to the surprise of some of its early investors. It was there that Steve Jobs, his sister and Steve Wozniak laboriously hand-assembled the first Apple 'computers' – in fact, just circuit boards. But that wasn't what Apple's first customer, Byte Shop's owner Paul Terrell, had ordered. He had made it clear that he expected fully assembled, complete computers ready to plug in for use. As Owen Linzmayer wrote in *Apple Confidential 2.0*,

> Terrell was a bit dismayed when Jobs showed up to deliver a batch of motherboards stuffed with components. Nonetheless, Terrell kept his word and handed over the cash, allowing Apple to pay off its parts suppliers with just one day to spare.[6]

Patty Jobs recalled that, even back then, her brother was a harsh taskmaster. He supervised her installation of computer chips on circuit boards. She recalled, 'I'd get yelled at if I bent a prong.'[7]

Originally, Paul Jobs had part of the garage set aside to rebuild cars for resale, but Apple took it over as well as a bedroom.

APPLE COMPUTER MOVES ON

Steve Jobs never thought it was odd to have his bootstrapped company operating out of a suburban garage. He knew of another start-up from Palo Alto, at 367 Addison Avenue, that went on to great success: industry giant Hewlett-Packard. (Years later, a garage in a residential home at Menlo Park would house another start-up called Google.)

Soon Apple outgrew the garage and rented suite B at an office building at 20833 Stevens Creek Boulevard, in Cupertino.

Apple moved again in 1978 to 10260 Bandley Drive.

Apple's current location is One Infinite Loop, also in Cupertino. Comprised of six buildings, the campus encompasses 850,000 square feet, with additional leased buildings throughout the city, bringing the total to 3.3 million square feet. The campus is affectionately called the Mothership. (Apple's gift shop is open to the public, unlike some companies that allow access only to employees. An Apple store favourite: a T-shirt that proudly proclaims, 'I visited the Mothership.')

THE SPACESHIP

Looking toward the future, Apple is building a new campus called Apple 2 one mile east of its current location to consolidate its offices and modernise in the process. It's anchored by an elegant glass structure designed by Norman Foster. When it's completed in 2016, the estimated $5 billion circular building with 2.82 million square feet will house thirteen thousand employees.

'It's a little like a spaceship,' Steve Jobs recalled.[8]

Dan Whisenhunt, Apple's senior director of real estate and facilities, said of the spaceship, 'You can be sure that, following Steve's lead, we've used the same care and the same meticulous attention to detail we put into every Apple product.'[9]

Where you start doesn't matter; what matters is where you end up.

6

Trust Life's Processes

'You have to trust in something.'

6

CONNECTING THE DOTS

IN HIS COMMENCEMENT ADDRESS, JOBS explained that 'you can't connect the dots looking forward; you can only connect them looking backwards. So you have to trust that the dots will somehow connect in the future.'[1] In other words, foresight is problematic, but insight can become apparent when viewed with the perspective of time.

Jobs is, in effect, saying: trust me. It'll all work out. There's a grand plan at work, but you just don't see it – yet.

Though Jobs did not make this comparison, another way to look at life is to consider it as an unassembled jigsaw puzzle. All the pieces are boxed, but you must take them out of the box, spread them out, look for patterns and assemble them. Slowly, as each new piece is inserted into place, a partial picture begins to emerge. But when enough pieces are assembled, a clearer picture can be seen. It's only by fully assembling the puzzle that it can be seen as a whole.

Jobs didn't agonise over whether he was doing the right thing or the wrong thing. He didn't pull out a notebook and make a timeline of his life, with markers to indicate goals. He didn't methodically plan his life with a daily organiser, to try to impose an artificial order on it. He didn't consciously 'punch the tickets' to success. Thinking like a Zen master, his plan for success was not to plan.

He simply lived his life by listening to himself and trusted that everything would work out in the end. He took to heart what Shakespeare's Hamlet said in Act 5, Scene 2: 'There's a divinity that shapes our ends, Rough-hew them how we will.'

Place your trust in life's processes, and let life run its course. In time all will become apparent.

SECOND STORY

Love and Loss

JOBS DISCOVERED THAT LOVE WAS WHAT GAVE life meaning: a love of fulfilling work, and a love for the people closest to him.

7

Find What You Love

'Don't settle.'

STEVE JOBS' PRESCRIPTION TO LIVING A FULL, satisfying work life is simply stated: 'You've got to find what you love.' That's what he told Stanford graduates. He never worked just to make money; instead, he shaped a career.

It's a working philosophy that others advocate, notably the late Joseph Campbell, who popularised the phrase 'Follow your bliss.' As he explained, 'There's a wise saying: make your hobby your source of income.'[1]

In Jobs' case, his hobby – dating back to high school – was electronics. As he told his official biographer, 'My friends were the really smart kids … I was interested in math and science and electronics.'[2]

THE GREAT AND POWERFUL WOZ

Those interests led his friend Bill Fernandez to introduce him to another Steve – Steve 'Woz' Wozniak, a fellow electronics geek. Woz recalled Bill telling him, 'Hey, there's someone you should meet. His name is Steve. He likes to do pranks like you do, and he's also into building electronics like you are.'[3]

The difference between the two was that Jobs was a hobbyist compared to Wozniak, an electronics wizard who knew he was 'meant to be an engineer who designs computers, an engineer who writes software … and an engineer who teaches other people things'.[4]

Woz recalls, 'Steve [Jobs] didn't ever code. He wasn't an engineer and he didn't do any original design, but he was technical enough to alter and change and add to other designs.'[5]

So what was Jobs' calling?

Jobs was a visionary who, like Walt Disney, envisioned the big picture to make things happen. Disney, in an observation that Steve Jobs might have made himself, said:

> I'm just very curious – got to find out what makes things tick – and I've always liked working with my hands; my father was a carpenter. I even apprenticed to my own machine shop here and learned the trade. Since my outlook and attitudes are ingrained throughout our organisation, all our people have this curiosity; it keeps us moving forward, exploring, experimenting, opening new doors.[6]

A PRODUCTIVE LIFE

Steve Jobs' career spanned thirty-four years. It formally began when incorporation papers were filed for Apple Computer on 3 January 1977 and ended on 24 August 2011, when Jobs hand-delivered a letter to the Apple board of directors stating that he was immediately stepping down as its CEO, albeit reluctantly.

During that long trip, Jobs' passion carried him through the good times and the bad times; the ups and downs in business cycles characteristic of business life.

What fuelled Jobs was the pleasure he had in creating great consumer products – not merely making money. When asked by an interviewer, 'What's it like to be rich?' Jobs responded, 'It wasn't that important, because I didn't do it for the money.'[7]

A WASTED LIFE

Jobs didn't want to live what Joseph Campbell called a 'Waste Land' life. Campbell said:

> [My impression] is that the majority of my friends are living Waste Land lives. In teaching, you have [students] who haven't come into the Waste Land yet. They're at the point of making the decision whether they're going to follow the way of their own zeal – the star that's dawned for them – or do what daddy and mother and friends want them to do.[8]

Campbell's observation enjoys renewed currency today, because of the emphasis placed on college students to find a practical major, such as accounting, math, computer science or the sciences in general.

In today's tight job market, and with the high cost of college tuition, does it make economic sense for students to 'follow the way of their own zeal' – or are they best advised to be practical and get a well-paying job?

Had Jobs followed conventional wisdom to travel a well-trod road to success, would we have ever seen the fruits of his creative labour? Unlikely.

An artist with a positive genius as a business visionary, Edwin Land of Polaroid believed that his company had to stand at the intersection of technology and the liberal arts. Jobs, who ensured that Apple had a similar ethos, said: 'It's in Apple's DNA that technology alone is not enough – it's technology married with liberal arts, married with the humanities, that yields us the result that makes our heart sing.'[9]

KNOWLEDGE VERSUS IMAGINATION

As Einstein famously said, 'Imagination is more important than knowledge.' Case in point: Knowledge gave us MS-DOS, Microsoft's operating system, but imagination gave us Apple's intuitive Mac OS, which was possible only when Jobs made an intuitive leap after seeing a computer demonstration at Xerox's Palo Alto Research Center (PARC).

Recognising a good idea when he saw it, Bill Gates copied Mac's graphical user interface to create Windows, which was better than MS-DOS, but clearly inferior to Mac's elegant interface. But it was Jobs who recognised the importance of the GUI when he first saw it at PARC. Later he said on PBS:

> The germ of the idea was there, and they did it very well. Within ten minutes, it was obvious to me that all computers would work like this someday. You couldn't argue about its inevitability, it was so obvious.[10]

~

'Talent,' wrote German philosopher Arthur Schopenhauer, 'is like the marksman who hits a target which others cannot reach; genius is like the marksman who hits a target, as far as which others cannot even see.'[11]

Simply put, Jobs was a business genius.

PIXAR

Most people know about Steve Jobs' lifelong interest in computers – the Apple II, the Mac, and the family of 'i' products,[12] such as iMac, iTunes, iPhone and iPad – but far fewer know the story behind his involvement in Pixar, which clearly spoke to his belief that you had to love your work because you're going to spend a lifetime doing it, and you may as well enjoy it instead of simply enduring it.

~

Lucasfilm's computer division would prove to be a dark horse, one that George Lucas was looking to put out to pasture.

Faced with a costly divorce from his wife, Marcia, Lucas had no interest in funding a fledgling operation whose not-so-hidden agenda was to create full-length computer-animated motion pictures. Lucas recalled, 'I couldn't really start another film company – I was already in the middle of one. We just didn't have the resources to try to put together an operation like that.'[13]

Lucas put Lucasfilm on the market in 1985 and asked for $15 million, which Jobs felt was too high, so he waited Lucas out. Needing cash, Lucas sold it to Jobs for $5 million. Jobs immediately put in another $5 million for operating capital and eventually sank $55 million into the company between 1986 and 1991.

Pixar's John Lasseter and Ed Catmull said that Jobs

> saw the potential of what Pixar could be before the rest of us, and beyond what anyone ever imagined. Steve took a chance on us and believed in our crazy dream of making computer animated films.[14]

Jobs was in it for the long haul. He had tried unsuccessfully to get Apple to buy the company earlier, because of its graphics capabilities, but Apple wasn't interested. So he made the investment himself.

In November 1995, nearly ten years after he bought the company, Pixar released *Toy Story* – the world's first computer-animated feature-length film.

Computer scientist Alan Kay was the person who suggested that Jobs buy the Lucasfilm computer division.[15] He was pleased Jobs took his advice, and observed:

> Steve just hung in there and hung in there and hung in there until they got into the sweet spot where everything that they knew suddenly was applicable in a way that made commercial sense.[16]

A practical businessman would have cut his losses long before the ten-year mark, and even Jobs had second thoughts:

> There were even a few times where I thought about selling it or getting another investor in. I got married, and my wife, Laurene, and I had started a family. When you're raising a family, you realise that at some point you've got to be sensible.[17]

But in the end, Jobs' persistence paid off. He stayed the course, and *Toy Story* went on to become a critical and financial success, grossing $361 million worldwide. It spawned two moneymaking sequels: *Toy Story 2* ($485 million worldwide gross) and *Toy Story 3* ($1 billion worldwide gross).

Apple, Inc. made Jobs a multimillionaire, but Pixar made him a billionaire. He sold the company in 2006 to Disney in exchange for stock, and with 50.1 per cent, he became the company's largest stockholder. As reported on CNET.com:

> Jobs said Pixar's main choices came down to selling out to Disney or working with another studio under a deal like Lucasfilm has with Twentieth Century Fox, in which the larger studio gets only a distribution fee. The latter option was somewhat attractive, Jobs said, but would still result in an arrangement with 'two companies with two separate sets of shareholders and two different agendas'.
>
> Disney is the only company with animation in their DNA, and the only company that we think has this incredible collection of unique assets like the theme parks, that are very attractive to us as well,' Jobs said on a conference call with investors. 'They're the only company who has Bob Iger, who we like a lot and have grown to trust.'[18]

In an introduction to an official history of Pixar, Jobs wrote: 'It's a great gift to be able to support yourself doing work that you love, and all of us have been honoured to see our characters and stories find a place in the world outside our studio.'[19]

Find the work that you love – and then relentlessly pursue it. That's where you will find your fortune.

8

Work Hard

'We worked hard, and in 10 years Apple had grown … into a $2 billion company with over 4000 employees.'

IN HIS COMMENCEMENT ADDRESS, STEVE JOBS cites hard work as a principle reason why Apple Computer was successful.

In looking back at his career, Jobs' work ethic proved to be a key to his success in all three 'acts' of his life: Apple Computer, NeXT and Pixar, and his triumphant return to Apple.

BEHIND THE SCENES

What people didn't see were the countless hours Jobs put in *behind* the scenes to make Apple successful. Interviewers eager to talk about each new sexy product had little interest in the mundane aspects of the business. They wanted to see the glitzy showroom, not the utilitarian backroom where the real work was being done.

For instance, when the two Steves started out, they spent countless man-hours assembling chips on a board to construct the Apple I. 'Before the Apple I,' recalled Wozniak, 'all computers had hard-to-read front panels and no screens and keyboards. After Apple I, they all did.'[1]

That romantic image of a bootstrapped start-up by two guys with a dream was at odds with reality: They bought parts on credit and then rushed to build the Apple I just in time to get paid from computer stores like the Byte Shop, which allowed them to pay off the suppliers. Jobs unknowingly took advantage of a Japanese manufacturing strategy called 'just in time' inventory, which matched supply with demand instead of stockpiling product in a warehouse.

Wozniak recalled that time with obvious affection:

> I was just the happiest person in the world … I never truly thought we were going to make money with Apple. That was never in my mind. The only thing on my mind was, Wow, now that I've discovered what a microprocessor can do, there are so many places I can take it. I knew that for the rest of my life, I would have a computing tool for myself.[2]

HARD DRIVE

In Apple's early years, work commanded virtually all of Jobs' attention. The demands of an undercapitalised start-up meant that while Wozniak focused on engineering responsibilities – designing the Apple I and then the Apple II – Jobs focused on sales and marketing. The two young men were perfect complements. They were both single and could focus all their attention on work.

MAC UNDER ATTACK

Both Steve Wozniak and Steve Jobs worked hard to make the Apple II a success, but they weren't the only beasts in the jungle. When IBM, the king of the jungle of the business world, woke up and saw the potential market for personal computers, Apple found itself with a formidable foe. IBM announced on 12 August 1981, that it was entering the fray: The giant ape bellowed and beat its hairy chest, and the other jungle beasts fled in fear.

Working to debut the Mac in January 1984, Jobs and his hand-picked team threw out the clock to set their own hours. As the days turned into weeks and then months, with the deadline fast approaching, the Mac team members put in all the time necessary to get the job done. To them, the Mac project was a dream, then a fevered dream, and finally a nightmare.

Jobs told *Playboy*, 'At Apple, people are putting in 18-hour days.' The justification, he explained, was that

> right now is one of those moments when we are influencing the future ... I think we have that opportunity now. And no, we don't know where it will lead. We just know there's something much bigger than any of us here.[3]

The Mac was their mission, their way to 'make a little dent in the universe' and change the world. That meant sacrifice, and if it meant working extraordinarily hard and long to get the job done, that was, all things considered, a small price for the Mac team to pay. The big picture, Jobs said, was what was important.

WHISTLE WHILE YOU WORK

Andy Hertzfeld, who worked on the Mac, recalls the hectic weeks just before the planned Mac debut.

> The absolute deadline for finishing the software was 6 a.m. on Monday, January 16, eight days before the introduction. When I came into work on Friday, January 13, I knew I would probably stay there all weekend, along with the rest of the team, working as hard as possible to shake out the remaining bugs before Monday …
>
> We finished with literally no time to spare, shipping the 'golden master' of the Write/Paint disc to the factory at 6 a.m. on Monday morning January 16, just a week before the introduction. By that point, most of the software team hadn't slept for days, so we all went home to collapse.[4]

The Mac team had accomplished what had been considered impossible – especially after software glitches that at one point were so pervasive that team members reluctantly went to Jobs to plead their case for more time.

Jobs exploded in anger. Known for taking infinite pains until everything was perfect, this time the deadline trumped perfection. 'No way, there's no way we're slipping! … Just make it as good as you can. You better get back to work!'[5]

~

When IBM debuted its personal computer on 12 August 1981, Apple ran an ad a day later in *The Wall Street Journal* welcoming the PC. Making it clear that Apple was there first ('When we invented the first personal computer system …'), the company nevertheless held out its hand to shake IBM's, an iron fist covered by a glove. Apple cheerfully said, 'We look forward to responsible competition in the massive effort to distribute this American technology to the world.'

Apple soon changed its tune when it realised that IBM wasn't taking any prisoners. Corporate America, which Apple wooed, saw Apple as an upstart, and it collectively upended the apple cart by rushing to the IBM PC platform. As the saying went, no purchasing agent was going to lose his job by buying an IBM product. The result: Fewer were now willing to take a bite of Apple, which was clearly technologically superior – but that would not be enough.

As Jobs' troops rallied around him, Jobs inflamed them with the idea that IBM was out to turn Apple into apple sauce. Taking the stage at an Apple shareholders meeting at Cupertino's Flint Center in January 1984, Jobs fired up the audience with a melodramatic speech – a classic good versus evil confrontation:

> In 1977, Apple, a young fledgling company on the west coast invents the Apple II, the first personal computer as we know it today. IBM dismisses the personal computer as too small to do serious computing and unimportant to their business ... It is now 1984. It appears IBM *wants it all.* Apple is perceived to be the only hope to offer IBM a run for its money. Dealers, initially welcoming IBM with open arms, now fear an IBM dominated and controlled future. They are increasingly turning back to Apple as the only force that can ensure their future freedom! IBM wants it all, and is aiming its guns to the last obstacle to industry control – Apple. Will Big Blue dominate the entire computer industry? The entire information age? Was George Orwell right?[6]

Apple then ran its famous 'George Orwell, 1984' ad that suggested IBM was Big Brother, out to control the world. Apple, its eyes wide open, now realised that IBM was in the game for keeps, and the winner takes all.

BACK TO THE DRAWING BOARD

Like the highly competitive computer industry, Hollywood's film industry was also high stakes poker: Because every feature film cost millions to produce and distribute, it could make or break executives' careers and, sometimes, film studios as well.

It's no wonder, then, that the head of Disney's film studio, Jeffrey Katzenberg, rode Pixar's executives hard, to the point of superimposing his vision of *Toy Story* over Lasseter's. When Katzenberg wanted the film to be edgy, more adult, Pixar's executives laboured mightily to meet his demands. But it was clear to them that Katzenberg's adulterated vision was out of focus for what was clearly a children's film that could stand, and be successful, on its own merits.

After diligently following specific directions from Katzenberg, Pixar's executive saw *Toy Story* morphing from an endearing story into a hard-edged, mean-spirited one. Even actor Tom Hanks, the voice of the cheery cowboy and leader, Woody, was surprised and expressed his concern. Hanks remarked, 'Wow, I never get to play characters like this. This guy's really a jerk!'[7]

The screening for Disney executives confirmed what the Pixar team had known to be the obvious truth: By trying too hard to please Disney's executives, they wound up pleasing no one – including themselves. After the screening, Disney gave the film a thumbs down. It was do-or-die time for Pixar, pressured by Disney's film executives to move key people to its Burbank studio where the production would be rebooted under their watchful eyes. That unpalatable prospect motivated Lasseter to give a pep talk to his troops.

> You know what? Let's just make the movie we want to make. We'll listen to their notes, but let's only take the ones we feel make the movie better and ignore the rest.[8]

It inspired them to go back to the drawing board and substantially rework it. 'We worked night and day,' recalled Pixar's Joe Ranft. And in the end they delivered the world's first full-length computer-animated film, and it proved to be a critical and financial success.[9]

THE END RESULT

Jobs' simple statement to the Stanford graduates – 'We worked hard' – was a dramatic understatement. It was in his nature to push himself and others to their limits – and then, by stretching, to infinity and beyond.

In the last phase of his life, when he returned to Apple to save it from being pulped, it took, as Jobs explained, 'a tremendous amount of work by a lot of people'.[10] But by rallying the troops, focusing, and persevering, Steve saved everybody's jobs.

To be successful, work hard; and when things get tough, work harder.

9

Seek Shared Visions

'How can you get fired from a company you started?'

IN THE BEGINNING, SCULLEY AND JOBS shared a common vision: John Sculley would join Apple as its CEO in April 1983, so that Steve Jobs could learn from him and, in time, grow into the position. But in the end, as Jobs described it, they had a spectacular falling out. Sculley won the power play. The executive selected by Jobs was ironically the same one who had a major hand in his expulsion from Apple. 'I hired the wrong guy. He destroyed everything I spent ten years working for, starting with me.'[1]

The February 1985 issue of *Playboy* included an 'Interview [with] 29-year-old zillionaire Steve Jobs of Apple Computers'. In its introduction, Jobs was described as

> the spirit of an entrepreneurial generation, the man to beat for now is the charismatic co-founder and chairman of

> Apple Computer, Inc., Steven Jobs. He transformed a small business begun in a garage in Los Altos, California, into a revolutionary billion-dollar company – one that joined the ranks of the Fortune 500 in just five years, faster than any other company in history.[2]

But only three months later, Steve Jobs left Apple and wouldn't return for twelve years.

What went so spectacularly wrong?

JOHN SCULLEY

As Sculley recalled, it began when Apple's board 'believed that Steve Jobs … was too inexperienced to take over' as CEO. Jobs himself agreed. Sculley was told by the board,

> [Jobs] wants to find someone who is really great who he can learn from. The new chief executive reports directly to the board. Steve is focused largely on product development.[3]

Apple hired Gerry Roche, a headhunter who felt Sculley was not only the best but the only person who fit the bill. Sculley, though, already had a promising career at PepsiCo – he was now its president and was short-listed to become its CEO.

Sculley agreed to meet with Jobs, and though their meetings were not formal interviews, it was clear that each was sizing the other up. Sculley found himself becoming more intrigued about the possibilities at Apple: Pepsi represented the old guard, Apple the new guard. But was it time for a sea change?

Sculley understandably had his misgivings. In his autobiography, *Odyssey*, he admitted: 'I don't know much about computers.' He later told Jobs, 'I'm not convinced it even makes sense to bring someone in from the soft-drink industry to run your company.'[4]

Jobs, though, had already convinced himself that it was either Sculley or no one. And the Apple board very much wanted a seasoned executive who would rein in Jobs, a maverick whose management style created churn in the Macintosh division. It had become Jobs' own fiefdom, at the expense of the Apple II division, which accounted for virtually all of the company's profits and whose employees felt marginalised: Mac was getting all the attention and the resources, but Apple II was keeping the boat afloat.

Once Jobs fixed an idea in his head, he never relinquished it. In this instance, Jobs relentlessly pursued and wooed Sculley.

Adding fuel to the fire, the headhunter hired by Apple had sung a siren song to Sculley about Silicon Valley, comparing it to how

> Florence might have been in the Renaissance. It's where all the bright minds are coming together and it's a place

> in time where wonderful things are going to happen … The geniuses of today aren't working on ceilings or marble, they're working on gallium arsenide chips and software. If Michelangelo were alive today, don't you think he would have been using some of these tools?[5]

Jobs was reaching out from Silicon Valley, and Sculley was reaching out from the buttoned-down culture of corporate America, East Coast–style. A planetary odd couple, they lived in disparate worlds that, eventually, would collide.

Sculley agreed to jump ship from Pepsi to take the helm at Apple. Jobs' reaction when Sculley called: 'You're coming? That's fantastic! That's incredible! This is the best day of my whole life!'[6] (The worst day of his whole life would come two years later, when he would find himself relieved of command of the Mac division as well as his executive vice president status.)

THE SHIP HITS AN ICEBERG

On 8 April 1983, Sculley was hired as Apple's CEO, and thc honeymoon between Jobs and Sculley began. Sculley dressed down, abandoning his corporate suit-and-tie uniform. The two were inseparable. 'Apple,' said Sculley, 'has one leader, Steve and me.'[7]

But from the time he came on board, Sculley, who saw computers principally as business tools, clearly lacked Jobs' vision. Sculley recalled, 'I could never figure out why someone would want a computer if he wasn't a hacker.'[8]

The simmering problem, though, eventually boiled over: Sculley's vision of his role at Apple and Jobs' vision of Sculley were worlds apart, and never the twain would meet. A business marriage made in heaven turned into hell a year later, and both knew it. The pair, termed the Dynamic Duo by the media, realised that divorce seemed inevitable. As Sculley recalled,

> It began when I told Steve that I was going to tell the board I didn't think he should be the general manager of the Macintosh division. I thought he ought to be the chairman and focus on setting the vision for the corporation. He should create the next base of technology and maybe lead a team that would build the next great products, as he had done with the Macintosh. This was back at the end of March 1985, when it was clear that the two of us were on a collision path.[9]

It would come to a head on 10 April 1985, when the board would meet to deal with the problem that had finally boiled over.

Once a friend and ally, Sculley was now Jobs' chief adversary. 'I wanted you here to help me grow, and you've been ineffective in helping me,' Jobs told Sculley at a board meeting with all hands present.[10]

The heart of the issue: Jobs wanted an active, hands-on role at Apple, which was not a realistic possibility.

After the board meeting, Jobs and Sculley took one of their last walks together, as they tried one final time to resolve the problem, but it was too late. The heart of the issue: How should the company be run? As Sculley recalled,

> Steve's view was that it had to be decentralised, because the only way to hold on to entrepreneurial-type people was to give them a chance to, in effect, run their own little business inside a large corporation. My sense was that a more overriding issue was to have one Apple. We were competing too much with ourselves. We had to have an organisational approach that would centralise the process of management by making sure that product development was working on building products for the marketplace and not competing with other parts of Apple.
>
> It came down to the level of confidence we had in each other. Steve didn't have confidence that I could run Apple, because he didn't think I knew enough about product operations. I didn't think he knew enough about operations and management. That's where the major disagreements were.[11]

The legal paperwork terminating Jobs as head of the Macintosh division was submitted on 31 May 1985. Steve Jobs was, as far as Apple was concerned, jobless, except for his position as chairman of the board: He was no longer a vice president, and no longer had any operational responsibilities as the Macintosh project manager.

It was a changing of the guard. Another Apple employee, unhappy with his largely ceremonial role at the company, decided it was also time to leave – Steve Wozniak, who saw himself not as an engineer per se but an artist, recalled,

> Most inventors and engineers I've met are like me – they're shy and they live in their heads. They're almost like artists. In fact, the very best of them *are* artists. *And artists work best alone* – best outside of corporate environments, best where they can control an invention's design without a lot of other people designing it for marketing or some other committee.[12]

It was the end of an era, the end of the innocence. Apple had grown, and there was no longer a place for the two Steves who cofounded the company.

THE SHIP TAKES ON WATER

Soon thereafter, Apple laid off twelve hundred employees – the first warning sign that the company was adrift. It was a sign of the times and a sign of what was to come: Apple's decision to part ways with both Steves would, in time, come back to haunt them – it would bring the company to the brink of extinction. It was increasingly apparent that keeping the company from going under was an ongoing challenge.

Sculley subsequently consolidated his power at Apple; he became not only its CEO but also its president. But it was clear to all that Apple had been coasting solely on Jobs' ideas. In *Star Trek* parlance, Apple jettisoned its warp core that powered its drive – Steve Jobs – and the company was now running on impulse power.

In retrospect, Apple's board of directors and Sculley should have worked closely with Jobs to help him understand CEO responsibilities; they should have put an appropriate training plan in place.

The root of the problem: Sculley's vision was not congruent with Jobs', and the two inevitably locked horns. Sculley wanted Jobs, who was the chairman of the board, to remain as 'a creator of powerful ideas and the champion of Apple's spirit'.[13] In other words, Jobs would have had no hands-on operational responsibilities.

THE SHIP SINKS

Years later, Sculley admitted he was a misfit at Apple:

> Looking back, it was a big mistake that I was ever hired as CEO. I was not the first choice that Steve wanted to be the CEO. He was the first choice, but the board wasn't

> prepared to make him CEO when he was 26 years old … I came in not knowing anything about computers. The idea was that Steve and I were going to work as partners. He would be the technical person and I would be the marketing person.
>
> … My sense is that when Steve left I still didn't know very much about computers … My decision was first to fix the company, but I didn't know how to fix companies and to get it back to be successful again.
>
> 'Steve, let's figure out how you can come back and lead your company.' I didn't do that. It was a terrible mistake on my part. I can't figure out why I didn't have the wisdom to do that. But I didn't. And as life has it, shortly after that, I was fired.[14]

Apple's board of directors was right in saying that Jobs had a lot to learn before he could take the reins as CEO. Only intensive hands-on training might have made Jobs an effective manager and leader.

But they instituted no such plan, and Jobs went off to start his own computer company. During that time he learned what he needed to know to become an effective CEO experientially instead of through a more formal teaching environment – the story of his life.

His obsession to hire Sculley at all costs cost Jobs his company. At the root of the problem: Sculley and Jobs were not looking in the same direction and thus had no shared vision.

In your life, personally and professionally, find people whose values you share, and whose vision matches your own.

10

Regain Focus

'What had been the focus of my entire adult life was gone.'

FOR STEVE JOBS, LEAVING HIS MAC OPERATIONS manager role at Apple was understandably a traumatic event. As Sculley recalled,

> Apple was Steve's whole life. It was almost impossible to separate the two personalities. Macintosh was like a son to Steve. And then to have the person he had brought in – I wouldn't have come here without Steve's persuasion – be the one who finally pushed him out was an incredibly difficult thing [for him] to handle.[1]

Steve Jobs went through the stages of grief. First, he denied the reality of the situation by bargaining with John Sculley, trying to find a place for himself operationally at Apple. Second, after failing to convince Sculley and the Apple board members to change their minds, Jobs isolated himself personally and professionally. Third, he vented his anger, smashing the inscribed photo Sculley had given him and leaving it behind in his former office; he would never speak to Sculley again, lashing out in the media at his former friend and mentor whom he now termed a 'bozo', an epithet he reserved for those he held in contempt. Fourth, he went through a period of dislocation marked by depression. And, finally, he came to accept that he couldn't change things as they were. He took off for France, Italy and Russia for a sabbatical for the summer, and didn't return to the United States until August 1985.

During that time he was able to do a lot of soul searching. He was thirty years old and wealthy, and he had the luxury of doing anything he wanted – except return to Apple in an operational capacity. He could travel the world, lecture to college students, be a consultant, set up a foundation, get involved in politics, or simply indulge himself in any way he chose. But none of those ideas appealed to him.

He was Apple to the core, even when he wasn't there in an active role. He was still the board chairman, but operationally he was part of the company's past and clearly not its future, according to the Apple board. Jobs was still a young man with a burning desire to make a dent in the universe. As he told *Playboy*,

> I'll always stay connected with Apple. I hope that throughout my life I'll sort of have the thread of my life and the thread of Apple weave in and out of each other, like a tapestry. There may be a few years when I'm not there, but I'll always come back. And that's what I may try to do.[2]

There would be time for looking back, but not now. It was time to look forward, to find his new place in the world. To do that, he had to focus on the things that he loved.

Known for his laserlike focus on any task at hand, Jobs was now adrift. His mental state recalled the text in a scroll designed as part of the first Apple logo: 'a mind for ever Voyaging through strange seas of Thought, alone.'[3]

Steve Jobs was truly alone.

ALL YOU NEED IS LOVE

The Mac had just come out, marking a sea change for personal computers. There were still opportunities for him, and still time, but not if he rested on his laurels.

He refocused his mind. Now it was time to get back to work.

What, he asked himself, should I do next?

~

Failure is life in disguise trying to teach you a lesson: Iterate until you get it right.

11

Start Over

'I was still in love. And so I decided to start over.'

JOBS SAID, WHEN HE WAS TWENTY-NINE AND still an operational manager at Apple,

> The key thing to remember about me is that I'm still a student. I'm still in boot camp. If anyone is reading any of my thoughts, I'd keep that in mind. Don't take it all too seriously. If you want to live your life in a creative way, as an artist, you have to not look back too much. You have to be willing to take whatever you've done and whoever you were and throw them away.[1]

THE FIRST STEP

It was now time for Jobs to write the first page to a new chapter in his playbook. It was time to go back to his roots – all the way back to the beginning, to the joy he found in working with Steve Wozniak when they created the iconic Apple II computer – and take what he learned at Apple to apply it to his next venture: a computer company called, naturally, NeXT.[2]

Apple's board presumed he'd stay in the computer industry; the board's only concern was the possibility of Jobs using Apple's proprietary information or technology.

It was after a conversation with Stanford biochemist Paul Berg that Steve Jobs realised he could design a new computer to fit a niche. Berg pointed out that conducting computer simulations in his field would require affordable workstations. But as he told Jobs, everything currently on the market was too expensive; moreover, current computers were underpowered for the task at hand.

The idea of a new, powerful workstation appealed to Jobs, because he had previously thought along those lines. Jobs once pushed at Apple the idea of just such a computer called the Big Mac. It would run not on the Mac operating system but on the more powerful UNIX operating system. But the idea never reached fruition.

Now the Big Mac could be built, but not for Apple Computer.

UP NEXT

In a letter dated 17 September 1985, to board member Mike Markkula, Jobs made a clean break. He asked that Apple accept his resignation as the board chairman, so he could start his new venture. He hoped the parting would be amicable.

'I am but 30,' he wrote, 'and want still to contribute and achieve.'

At NeXT, he could fulfil his dream to build a computer powerful enough to run the complex simulations required by universities. But as its features and capabilities grew, so did its cost, until it became prohibitively expensive. As Walter Isaacson wrote in *Steve Jobs*,

> his panel of academic advisors had long pushed to keep the price to between $2,000 and $3,000, and they thought that Jobs had promised to do so. Some of them were appalled [at the $6,500 price]. This was especially true once they discovered that the optional printer would cost another $2,000, and the slowness of the optical disk would make the purchase of a $2,500 external hard drive advisable.[3]

In the end, NeXT sold only fifty thousand computers, not enough to keep its doors open. NeXT left the hardware business behind to focus on its crown jewel, its software, which would later find the unlikeliest buyer – Apple.

Up next: Pixar.

PICTURE PERFECT: PIXAR

Hardware, Jobs felt, had its limitations: It was here today, gone tomorrow. Bill Gates of Microsoft shares that view, which is why it's largely been a software company, as Steve Ballmer, its ex-CEO, explained: 'The name of the company is Micro*soft*. Micro … *soft*. It was a fundamental part of the founding principles: we were a software company.'[4]

But technology carries within the destructive seeds of obsolescence, said Jobs, who considered it ephemeral, whereas art has staying power.

> Creating technology is like laying down a sedimentary layer – layers of sediment that will support what others build above it, but that nobody will ever see again once they do. Pixar's work is very different. People will still be watching Pixar's films a hundred years from now, just as they watch *Snow White*, a 75-year-old movie, today. I guess that's the difference between art and technology.[5]

Purchased from George Lucas on 3 February 1986, for far less than the original asking price, Pixar – then known as the computer division of Lucasfilm – would be a black hole in terms of Jobs' investment dollars for the next decade.

Jobs, who sold his Apple stock in a depressed market to finance NeXT and purchase Pixar, soon found himself writing big cheques, with too little to show for it. Haemorrhaging money, a despondent Jobs at one time shopped Pixar around to prospective buyers, including Microsoft. But there were no buyers.

In the end Jobs decided to keep it going; he kept the faith, long after other investors would have bailed.

What did Jobs see in Pixar to justify such long-term commitment?

'Pixar,' said Jobs,

> was like a big hill to climb for the first ten years, always uphill, no rest, no plateau, just always uphill. But then, with *Toy Story* it became a wonderful success, surprising everyone, and it's been nothing but fun since then.[6]

Had Jobs still worked at Apple, George Lucas likely would have sold the company to someone else who may not have necessarily shared the long-range vision that the co-founders, Ed Catmull and Alvy Ray Smith, held: to make feature-length computer-animated films.

But Pixar was a long way from releasing such a film. The early years were spent making critically successful short films, on which the company cut its teeth; and besides, Pixar had no relationship with a major Hollywood studio, which was essential for distributing a feature-length film because of the costs involved.

~

Jobs found himself worried about cash flow and money. As he said,

> Pixar was a money pit for me. I kept putting more money into it, and the only bright spot was John's [Lasseter] short films. He'd say, Can I have $300,000 to make a short film? And I'd say okay, go make it. That was the only thing that was fun. Everything else was not really working.[7]

Jobs always loved the idea of upending an industry by improving it, and the time for computer animation had come. The traditional way to make a full-length animated film was with hand-drawn animation, but computer animation gives pictures a distinctive, appealing look. Furthermore, Jobs loved the idea of once again working with teams of creative people who shared his uncompromising vision. As always, the Holy Grail was product excellence, which was always time-consuming and expensive. But Jobs felt it was the only path to take.

Like Walt Disney, Jobs was more an impresario than anything else. Like Disney, he knew that working with creative people was like herding cats, and he knew it was best to let an experienced cat herder like John Lasseter do that job because creative people as a group can be difficult.

Steve Jobs' principal role, then, was to keep writing the cheques and being the face of Pixar to corporate America. The cheques were critical: Computer animation was expensive. Even a short, which ran a few minutes, could cost hundreds of thousands of dollars. And *Toy Story*, Pixar's first feature-length film, cost $30 million to produce.

PIXAR TODAY

In 2010 Pixar celebrated its twenty-fifth birthday.

Jobs, who lived long enough to see its success, had trusted his instincts and invested in a company that no one else would. And his films went on to gross $3.3 billion domestically and $7.7 billion worldwide.[8]

He found what he loved, funded it and watched it grow beyond all expectations.

Reinvent your life. Start living or start dying.

12

Keep the Faith

'Sometimes life hits you in the head with a brick. Don't lose faith.'

LOOKING BACK OVER JOBS' CAREER, WE CAN see how the negative decisions and experiences in his life were turned into positive ones, because he accepted them.

A prominent example of an acknowledged business failure: Thousands of $10,000 Lisa computers were trashed, buried in a landfill in Utah overseen by armed guards. Lisa was a failure, though earlier Jobs had been its chief advocate. 'We're going to blow IBM away,' he'd told John Sculley enthusiastically. 'There's nothing they can do when this computer comes out. This is so revolutionary, it's incredible.'[1]

But Lisa was too expensive for the business market, in addition to performance issues that doomed it. Alan Kay, an Apple fellow,[2] explained, 'The Lisa failed because it was very under-powered, and so while it did beautiful things, it did them very slowly.'[3]

We celebrate Steve Jobs' successes, but in order for him to succeed, he had to fail, learn from his mistakes, and keep the faith. Only then could Jobs grow personally and professionally.

PERSONAL FAILURE

He dropped out of college and failed to get a degree ... but what he learned when auditing classes and what he learned on the job – at Apple, NeXT, and Pixar – gave him an excellent, worldly education.

He initially and deliberately failed as a father to his daughter Lisa, by a previous relationship, whom he abandoned in her early years ... but he later accepted and took care of her and became the father he was meant to be.

He was deeply in love with Tina Redse, proposed to her, and got rejected because she felt that although they had much in common, their differences would eventually sabotage a marriage ... but he later met, and married, Laurene Powell, who proved to be the love of his life.

He failed to be a successful operational manager for the Macintosh division ... but when he eventually returned to Apple, he rallied the troops, hand-picked an excellent management team, and rebuilt the company from the ground up.

He championed the Apple III, which, as Wozniak said, 'just wasn't a good enough machine and it had so many flaws from the start that when we reintroduced it we should have called it the Apple IV.'[4] After losing $60 million on the computer, Apple was forced to shut it down and rethink how it would enter the business market to combat IBM's personal computer.

The powerful Lisa computer, which was designed specifically for the business community, never met sales expectations and was quietly discontinued … but with it gone, the company was able to focus on the Macintosh for 1984.

The stunningly designed Power Mac G4 Cube caught everyone's eye and prompted Jobs to exclaim that it was 'simply the coolest computer ever'.[5] It failed to sell, though, because 'it was too expensive, not powerful enough, and hard to upgrade'.[6] But its emphasis on pure design became Apple's industrial signature.

The expensive NeXT computer never found its niche … but its UNIX-based operating system would be Jobs' ticket to ride back to Apple, and be the core of the next generation of Mac computers.

'Don't settle,' he urged Stanford graduates. He never did. He never set out to fail, but he also never failed to learn from his mistakes, move on, and create the next insanely great product.

He did that by keeping the faith.

Keep your dream alive by keeping the faith – be reborn like a phoenix rising.

13

Save Face

'I was a very public failure.'

UNWANTED MEDIA SCRUTINY

THE UPSIDE TO BEING STEVE JOBS, ESPECIALLY in the wake of the Mac's release, was that he got all the media coverage he wanted. But the downside is that, when things took a bad turn, he got all the media coverage he *didn't* want.

To the world at large, and especially within the computer industry, Jobs was like Icarus, who dared to fly too high, only to fall earthward. Jobs, whose testy nature made for tempestuous relationships, especially with the press, found himself on the receiving end of unflattering coverage. In Silicon Valley, when the news broke, schadenfreude was inevitable: Jobs had alienated too many people over the years, and now it was payback time. His critics, peers and the media at large piled up on him with glee.

As Jobs told the Stanford graduates, he considered himself such a failure that he thought about leaving Silicon Valley.

No matter where Jobs went locally, he metaphorically wore a scarlet 'A' for Apple. He knew that, as a recognisable public figure, people would point and talk about him. He was famous, which he realised was a dual-edged sword. He was exposed, metaphorically walking naked in the world, and he wanted to hide. People stared.

But neither hiding and licking his wounds in Silicon Valley nor fleeing the country was his style. An internationally known figure, Jobs would forever be tethered to Apple Computer because he was a co-founder; moreover, his personality prevented him from retiring to live the lifestyle of the rich and famous.

He could run but he could not hide.

At the time, faced with a barrage of bad publicity and with the sure knowledge that his contemporaries were well aware of his fall from grace, Jobs had two choices: Slink away and become a rich recluse, as Howard Hughes did, or man up and take back control of his life.

'And so I decided to start over,' he told the Stanford graduates.

Don't play the blame-and-shame game – just prove your critics wrong.

14

Make Time Enough for Love

'You've got to find what you love.'

14

THERE'S A CLARITY THAT COMES WHEN you know the end of your life is drawing near. It's the time when those closest to you are there to surround you with their love.

Everything in life shrinks down to the one room that you occupy, with the sure knowledge that all that remains is passing on and passing over.

Steve Jobs told Stanford graduates that 'getting fired' from Apple gave him the opportunity to start two new companies; he also met the woman he eventually married during that time. Together, they had three children: Reed, Erin and Eve. (With a former girlfriend, he also had a daughter named Lisa, a Harvard graduate and magazine writer.)

On his deathbed, Jobs surrounded himself with family: his wife, Laurene; his four children; his biological sister, Mona Simpson; and his adoptive sister, Patty. They were the ones he would regretfully leave behind.

What most people, and certainly his critics, recall about Steve Jobs is that he was an extraordinarily difficult man to work and live with, which he freely admitted. That side of him got a lot of press, mostly bad. But there was a gentler side of him that rarely got press coverage, which he kept from the klieg lights that illuminated the rest of his life.

In a poignant eulogy for her brother, with whom she spoke nearly every other day for as long as they had known each other, Mona Simpson revealed that he was a romantic at heart. 'Steve,' she wrote,

> was like a girl in the amount of time he spent talking about love. Love was his supreme virtue, his god of gods … He believed that love happened all the time, everywhere.[1]

Because he believed in true love, he never gave up searching for it and eventually found it when he was thirty-six years old. Ironically, after a lifetime of looking for it, he found it when he wasn't looking. The woman in question, Laurene Powell, had walked into his life, changing it forever. She was the Beauty who finally tamed the Beast.

PICTURE THIS

Steve Jobs told photographer Diana Walker that one of his favourite portraits was a black-and-white photo of him and Laurene on the lawn of their home in Palo Alto, taken in August 1997. Laurene's eyes are closed and Steve is smiling. It's a beautiful photo, and an emotional one, but the one that plucks our heartstrings was made by Lea Suzuki, taken at an Apple public event in June 2011. In it we see Steve and Laurene in profile. Steve, bald with thinning hair, is obviously gaunt; Laurene's long blonde hair cascades around her shoulders. Their eyes are closed, and Steve has leaned forward; their foreheads are touching. Surrounded by men in suits, they are oblivious, lost in their own world, in a private moment that no one would dare to intrude on.

That photo was taken only three months before Steve Jobs died. In it we can see that after twenty years of marriage, they were like newlyweds, still very much in love.

What, one asks, kept him going from the time he was diagnosed in 2003 with a tumour until his death in 2011?

'His abiding love for Laurene sustained him,' said Mona Simpson when she spoke at his memorial service.

~

Jobs was well known for his lack of empathy. At Apple and NeXT, he vigorously opposed giving severance pay for soon-to-be laid-off employees and never hesitated to fire people. Back then, Jobs considered it just business, not personal.

But years later, in May 2003, he told students at Stanford's Graduate School of Business:

> When I was younger, and I had to fire someone, I didn't think twice about it. Even if [he] has really screwed up

> and some[one] else should have fired him last year, you need to remember that he's going to have to go home and tell his wife and kids that he's been fired and no longer has a job.[2]

What Jobs rarely shared during talks with students was that his infamous temper frequently led to screaming matches. It was his way of dealing with people he considered to be bozos – his most derogatory term, which recalls a popular clown of the same name.

In the book *The Pixar Touch*, David Price cited an instance when Jobs got into a screaming match with a Pixar executive, Ed Smith, who recalled, 'He went crazy on me and started insulting my accent ... We're screaming at each other, and our faces are about three inches apart.'[3]

PERSONAL LIFE

As a matter of policy, Steve Jobs carefully avoided discussing his personal life in interviews, preferring to talk only about his new products.

Steve Jobs didn't know who his biological mother was and later repudiated his biological father. The result was that after Clara Jobs died in 1986, he was left with only one parent – his adoptive father, Paul Jobs (who died in 1993).

Curious about the identity of his biological mother, Jobs hired a detective in the mid-eighties to locate her. Not long afterward, Jobs discovered that his biological mother was Joanne Simpson (maiden name: Schieble).

What Jobs didn't know was that his biological father also had a daughter with Joanne after Steve was put up for adoption. Jobs' sister, Mona, though, took the surname of Simpson, after her mother's second husband (Jandali abandoned his wife and daughter – the reason Steve repudiated him). For Jobs, having a blood sibling with whom he could talk was a novel idea.

Steve and Mona met through their mother when he was in his early thirties. Their relationship stood the test of time, ending only with his death twenty-five years later. In a touching eulogy for her sibling, Mona Simpson wrote that 'my whole life I'd been waiting for a man to love, who could love me … When I was 25, I met that man and he was my brother.'

The love was mutual. Steve Jobs shared a special connection with her that both acknowledged. As Jobs told *The New York Times*, 'She's one of my best friends in the world. I call her and talk to her every couple of days.'[4]

Brother and sister, they shared their lives and held onto each other tenaciously. 'Steve had been successful at a young age, and he felt that had isolated him.'[5]

To whom could he talk? To whom could he pour out his heart? Who could he be with and not be judged? Mona, who accepted him for who he was, warts and all, and didn't care that he was rich or famous or a celebrity – she just *cared.*

SPIRITUAL SOUL: TINA REDSE

Handsome and charismatic, Steve Jobs, when he chose to do so, could turn on his irresistible charm, and women were flattered. He was famous, rich and young. What was there not to like?

When he was single, finding women to date wasn't the problem; getting them to stay was the problem. Jobs, famous for his volatile personality, was hard on the women he dated, just as he was with the people with whom he worked. It made for passionate but tumultuous relationships.

Of all the women that he dated before he got married, one stood out – Christina 'Tina' Redse, a pretty blonde with long hair. They both sensed that their relationship was unique. They felt there was a special spiritual connection between them that was undeniable, a sentiment Jobs expressed even after he was married.

It was Redse who joined Jobs on a trip to France after his acrimonious split from Apple. She was also the first woman whom he loved enough to propose to – only to be turned down. They both clearly loved each other, but she was wise enough to realise that their marriage would likely end in divorce, because their personalities too often clashed.

Steve Jobs clearly loved Redse, and she loved him. But love was not enough. As Joseph Campbell points out in *An Open Life*, marriage is about both parties surrendering themselves to a third entity – the relationship itself.

Though they would each go on to marry someone else, Redse remained a strong presence – albeit at a distance – until the end of Jobs' days. They both knew that their relationship *was* special in many ways; it just wasn't strong enough to survive the rigours of marriage. A realist, Tina Redse knew that she was the one who had to walk away from the hopeless romantic, who dated extensively but truly loved only two women in his lifetime.

SOUL MATE: LAURENE POWELL

'You've got to find what you love,' Jobs told the Stanford graduates; he meant not only life's work but love in interpersonal relationships.

Jobs met his wife through a happy coincidence. At an evening lecture at Stanford Business School, Laurene Powell took a seat in the front row; to her right, the speaker took his seat when he arrived. The speaker was Steve Jobs.

After the lecture, Jobs caught up with her in the parking lot and proposed they go out right then for a dinner date, preempting a scheduled dinner engagement with NeXT employees. It was a spontaneous gesture, a romantic one, and Laurene Powell agreed.

Though Jobs credited getting fired for giving him the opportunity to meet Powell – in other words, he took a divergent path that led to her – it would have come to nothing if he wasn't finally ready to enter that relationship. Through all of his experiences, his essential nature remained unchanged: his prickly personality, his quirks and his uncompromising vision of the world. But perhaps the intervening years mellowed him ... somewhat.

As for Laurene, this one, Jobs knew, was special. He fell in love with her ... and never fell out of love. Their relationship would stand the test of time. As he said, 'It was tough, but you eventually realise you've met the person, you know, who you're right to live with.'[6]

The second time around, older and wiser, Steve Jobs would be a much better father to his children with Laurene than he was to Lisa. Time, though, remained at a premium: work came first, and the children got a piece of whatever remained.

Their three children – Reed, Erin and Eve – live as normal a life as possible by design, in a large but not extravagant home in Palo Alto. Though wealthy, Steve and Laurene didn't want to live a corresponding lifestyle, like some of their contemporaries. The Jobs' suburban home measures approximately six thousand square feet. Both Steve Jobs and Laurene Powell felt less was more: They didn't need to surround themselves with things, though they could afford everything; they surrounded themselves with their children and a simple lifestyle that suited them.

Steve remained married to Laurene for the rest of his life. They would share over two decades together, growing together, surrendering to each other, becoming a true marriage of minds, as seen in a love note he wrote to her:

> We've been through so much together and here we are right back where we started 20 years ago – older and wiser – with wrinkles on our faces and hearts. We now know many of life's joys, sufferings, secrets and wonders and we're still here together. My feet have never touched the ground.[7]

A lifelong romantic with the soul of a poet, a man who loved Shakespeare, Bob Dylan and Dylan Thomas, Steve Jobs lived to see life come full circle. In the last phase of his life, he didn't walk alone. His life, he realised, started out as a solitary journey but ended up as a shared journey with his wife at his side, holding his hand, flanked by their children.

Jobs lived what Joseph Campbell defined as a true marriage: 'A marriage is a commitment to that which you are. That person is literally your other half. And you and the other are one.'[8]

~

You can't find love; instead, open your heart and let it find you.

15

Create Great Products

'... the only way to do great work is to love what you do.'

THE FOUNDER OF AN ADVERTISING AGENCY bearing his name, David Ogilvy famously said, 'The consumer isn't a moron; she is your wife.' In other words, don't treat your customers as if they're fools; treat them with respect.

It's a lesson that was lost to Apple Computer after Steve Jobs left, because the CEOs of the company were adrift. They were like deckhands shuffling chairs on the *Titanic* as it kept taking on water.

First, John Sculley foundered:

> I did not have the breadth of experience at that time to really appreciate just how different leadership is when you are shaping an industry, as Bill Gates did or Steve Jobs did, versus when you're a competitor in an industry, in a public company, where you don't make mistakes because if you lose, you're out.[1]

He was then replaced by Michael Spindler, whose answer to Apple's financial problems was to try to sell the company outright to the computer company Sun Microsystems or to Philips, a multinational electronics company. Spinning out of control, Spindler was fired, and Gil Amelio, who was brought in, was shocked at what he saw:

> When I arrived, Apple was manufacturing the wrong products, with the wrong features, in the wrong quantities, marred with severe quality problems. The warehouses were stuffed with $600 million worth of unsaleable computers. The hard cash reserves were so low that the company could not survive more than another four months. Executives made decisions based on what was right for their own operation, not on what was right for the company. And the culture stressed the individual and freedom of action instead of cooperation and working toward a set of common goals.[2]

ROW, ROW, ROW YOUR BOAT

At a cocktail party in 1996, Amelio was overheard saying that Apple was no longer shipshape.

> Apple is a boat. There's a hole in the boat, and it's taking on water. But there's also a treasure on board. And the problem is, everyone on board is rowing in different directions,

> so the boat is just standing still. My job is to get everyone rowing in the same direction so we can save the treasure.[3]

Someone at the party then asked: 'But what about the hole?'

~

Apple, in imminent danger of going under, desperately needed a captain to take the helm and plug up the hole, right the ship and steer a new, profitable course. Clearly Sculley, Spindler and Amelio were not the captains of industry the Apple board had hoped they would be.

Reenter Steve Jobs, dubbed the comeback kid.

In the end, it came down to the numbers and a matter of probability. The board determined that if things continued on their current course, there was a high probability that Apple would go out of business in the short term. But if Steve Jobs took the helm, the probability was higher that the company would survive and in time perhaps even become profitable again.

Apple stock was down to its all-time low of $3.16 a share on 1 July 1997. It was losing $1 billion a year, with the company's market cap at $3 billion.

The board wisely voted to bring Jobs back. Only then would Apple begin its slow climb to profitability. Two years earlier, Jobs gave an interview in which he expressed grave concerns. 'Apple's on a glide slope to dying.'[4]

Jobs' prescription to turn things around: 'All that matters is the work.'[5] But the products had to be great, which takes time.

GOLDEN APPLES

It was time for Apple to reclaim its mojo and stop treating customers as morons who'd buy anything with an Apple label attached. As *Macworld*'s Colin Crawford recalled, '[Jobs] said that Apple's brand was badly tarnished and that he intended to repolish it.'[6]

Jobs, with a prior commitment to Pixar, initially demurred to become Apple's CEO in July 1997. Instead he became Apple's interim CEO (iCEO) and subsequently took the helm as CEO in late 1997. He then took immediate, drastic action: He asked for all but one of the board members to resign, so he could install a new team; he merged the overlapping product lines into four functional categories; and he simplified the number of product offerings.

Redesigning the Apple product line, Jobs' grand vision was to unify consumer products with the computer as its hub, and new products as its spokes. The computer would be powered by a new, UNIX-based operating system.

In 2001, the iPod replaced compact disc players; in 2003, the iTunes Store, where digital music could be bought and downloaded, gave consumers a legitimate, and virus-free, alternative to illegal downloads. In 2007, the iPhone replaced primitive mobile phones; and in 2010, the iPad proved to be a popular alternative to netbooks.

In March 2014, an Apple share sold for $530, and the company's market cap was $473 billion.

How did Jobs do it?

He did it by doing what he did best: creating great products, no matter how much time it took to get them right. It was his core business philosophy, dating back to 1977, when the Apple II was released. Seven years later, when Jobs debuted the Macintosh, the Mac team wore silkscreened T-shirts to proclaim the increasing number of hours they worked. Jobs even proclaimed to the media that they were indeed working '90 hours a week' and had T-shirts stating so – a fanciful exaggeration.

But the Mac team often burned the midnight oil, as Mac software engineer Andy Hertzfeld explained:

> Most of the Macintosh software team members were between twenty and thirty years old, and with few family obligations to distract us, we were used to working long hours ... By the fall of 1983, it wasn't unusual to find most of the software team in their cubicles on any given evening, week day or not, still tapping away at their keyboards at 11 p.m. or even later.[7]

Jobs was one of them in age and marital status. He orchestrated his rebels with a cause like a maestro, and together the Mac team felt they were on a holy mission.

But times change, and the brash twenty-eight-year-old was now forty-two years old. No longer just the operational head of the Mac division, Jobs was saddled with significant responsibilities: He was a dual CEO (Apple in Cupertino and Pixar in Point Richmond), and he was wearing himself thin, like too little butter scraped over too much toast.

AN ARTIST'S SENSIBILITIES

Looking back, Jobs' nonexistent academic and professional credentials made him an unlikely candidate to put such a large dent in the universe, as a *Time* magazine article pointed out:

> Steve Jobs remade the world as completely as a single human being ever has, but he had no business doing it. He wasn't qualified. He wasn't a computer scientist. He had no training as a hardware engineer or an industrial designer. He had a semester at Reed College and a stint at an ashram in India. Jobs's expertise was less in computers than it was in the humans who used them.[8]

Measured by a conventional yardstick, if the unconventional Jobs were to seek a job today at Google, Facebook or Microsoft, he'd likely be rejected by the human resources department. Steve need not apply for any jobs. Come back, they'd likely say, when you have a piece of paper from a college or university to prove you have an education.

But Jobs considered himself an artist whose sensibilities imposed their own demands. Those sensibilities made him unique, instead of being a credentialed professional working in a narrow field. He saw the big picture in a way that others could not.

Jobs' strengths:

- He drew inspiration not only from the technical world of computers but also from the liberal arts. He existed in both worlds.
- He had a laserlike focus on any task at hand.
- He worked only on products for which he had a great passion.
- He didn't put his faith just in the idea; instead, he focused on its flawless execution.
- He was quick to say no because he knew that you can't do everything well – just a select few.
- He placed his faith in Eastern, not Western, thinking; he valued intuition over rationality, flexibility over dogmatism, and the experiential over the empirical.
- His designs fused beauty with functionality: form married with function.
- He drew inspiration from the natural world. He didn't invent things but reinvented them.
- He believed in Leonardo da Vinci's notion that 'simplicity is the ultimate sophistication'.[9] He saw that in Zen philosophy and in the Japanese sensibility.

- He focused on the smallest details, which others overlooked.
- The bottom line: He focused on the customer experience.

IPOD: MUSIC TO MY EARS

Consider the iPod. Released on 23 October 2001, the portable MP3 music player's catchy ad slogan, created by TBWA/Chiat/Day, promised that it 'puts 1,000 Songs in Your Pocket'.

When Steve Jobs introduced the iPod, he explained that

> Apple has invented a whole new category of digital music player that lets you put your entire music collection in your pocket and listen to it wherever you go. With iPod, listening to music will never be the same again.[10]

Weighing only 184 grams, the iPod had a 5-gigabyte hard drive and played up to ten hours of continuous music. Apple's PR department explained that

> Apple has applied its legendary expertise in human interface engineering to make iPod the easiest to use digital device ever. Simply rotate iPod's unique scroll-wheel with your thumb or finger to quickly access your entire music collection by playlists, artists or songs.[11]

In 2001, the iPod was compatible only with the Mac computer. In 2002, the second-generation iPod held four times as many songs and was compatible with Windows as well. And in 2003, Apple launched the iTunes Store with individual songs uniformly priced at ninety-nine cents each.

Iterating with each new generation of iPod, in 2007 Apple added the iPod Touch to its line, with the capability of running small programs called 'apps'. By 2010, more than a quarter million apps were available for its platform. By then 275 million iPods had been sold. And in February 2013, Apple announced that 25 billion songs had been sold, with over 40 billion app downloads.

Apple's iPod was now the proverbial 800-pound gorilla in the music room.

ZUNE: OUT OF TUNE

In 2006 Microsoft Corporation released with great fanfare its answer to the iPod. An enthusiastic Bill Gates explained, 'Zune is a big investment for us. It's a vision that will carry us forward for years.'[12]

Zune entered the market and captured only 9 per cent of the market share at a time when Apple had 63 per cent.

Microsoft's big investment, as it turned out, was a false note. Up against the firmly entrenched and far superior iPod, the Zune lasted only three years before Microsoft reluctantly admitted defeat, which was duly noted by the media at large.

'It's the end of the road for a name that once symbolised Microsoft's grand plans to curb Apple's entertainment ambitions,' wrote Nick Wingfield of *The New York Times.* 'The Zune was a failure in the market, coming too late to stop the iPod juggernaut and falling short of the high bar Apple had set.'[13]

Microsoft's principal failing was that it didn't innovate – it imitated but failed to improve on the original.

Tony Fadell, who invented the iPod, explained the difference between the two companies:

> If you're a company focused on competitors, you'll be a follower. And you'll talk to the media about all sorts of stuff. But if you're a company focused on the consumer, you'll talk about the products that you've got and how to get the most out of them. But you won't talk about what's coming and you won't talk strategy. Consumers are interested in products.[14]

You are meant to do great work. Make it so.

16

Don't Settle

'So keep looking.'

IN BUSINESS, THE TEMPTATION TO SETTLE FOR less is always present. Under pressure to deliver, under financial constraints to cut costs to maximise profits, and under time constraints because the client or customer always needs it yesterday, it's easy to justify cutting corners and settling for less. But for Jobs, it was a surefire prescription for creating bozo products and services.

Early on, Jobs realised that there was only one way to do a job: Do it right the first time, from start to finish.

As he told *Playboy*:

> When you're a carpenter making a beautiful chest of drawers, you're not going to use a piece of plywood on the back, even though it faces the wall and nobody will ever see it. You'll know it's there, so you're going to use a beautiful piece of wood on the back. For you to sleep well at night, the aesthetic, the quality, has to be carried all the way through.[1]

It's a simple idea but difficult to execute consistently in the business world where external pressures force your hand, whether you like it or not.

Steve Jobs saw external justifications for what they were – excuses invoked in the name of expediency. Achieving product perfection meant never compromising. It was a constant thread that ran through the tapestry of his life.

From numerous examples, here are three.

THE CLONE WARS: CHEAP KNOCKOFFS

When Jobs was forced from Apple, the executives decided to lease the crown jewel, its operating system, to other companies, who would create Mac clones and pay a commission for each computer sold.

Under Jobs, the Mac OS was available only with a Mac. Jobs' central idea was that to ensure the customer experience was outstanding, software and hardware had to be seamlessly integrated in a great product.

But by allowing other companies to make Mac clones, which directly competed with Apple's own products, quality control was an issue. Moreover, the clones ate into Apple's profits on computer sales, which Apple's executives, suffering from a failure of imagination, failed to see. Jobs would have told them that selling out your product to make a quick buck cheapens your brand.

When Jobs returned to Apple, one of the first things he did was to kill the existing contracts with the computer clone companies. As he later explained, had he not done so, 'Apple would have a very hard time returning to profitability, and it would drag down the whole Mac ecosystem.'[2]

PICTURE IMPERFECT: THE SCHEDULE IS BOSS

On the heels of *Toy Story*'s success, Disney wanted to follow up with a direct-to-video film, so Pixar pitched *Toy Story 2* as a lower-budget production, secondary to its current project, *A Bug's Life*, a major theatrical release. But as *Toy Story 2* developed, Pixar realised that it was better suited for a feature-length film, and successfully pitched that idea to Disney.

It meant Pixar would be working on two major film releases simultaneously, which they had never done before. At the time they had no inkling the toll it would take on their staff and resources.

Disney, meanwhile, forged ahead with its promotional and marketing plans for *Toy Story 2*. The company lined up toy licences and promotional plans based on the expectation that in nine months Pixar would turn in a completed film ready for theatrical release.

But after watching *Toy Story*, Lasseter went into the office the next day to see what had been done on *Toy Story 2*, and realised that in rushing to meet Disney's deadline, the film didn't meet his expectations; if released, *Toy Story 2* would tarnish Pixar's reputation.

Lasseter immediately brought it up to Disney's executives, who made it clear to him that their train was going to get to the station on time, and as its conductor, Lasseter was responsible for making that happen. Lasseter had made a promise, Disney had acted on that promise, and Disney expected Pixar to deliver. End of story.

As Tom Schumacher, a former Disney president who oversaw animated features, explained:

> John and I were sitting at the table with some of my Disney colleagues, who said, 'Well, it's okay.' And I can't imagine anything more crushing to John Lasseter than the expression, 'Well, it's okay.' It's just unacceptable to him, and it's one of his most endearing, most exasperating qualities, and probably the biggest reason for his success. That was just death to him, that these characters would end up in a movie that was 'just okay'. So nine months before it was supposed to come out, John threw the vast majority of the movie out and then started over. Which is *unheard of.*[3]

Like his boss Steve Jobs, Lasseter never settles for less, and immediately broke the news to the staff: It's all hands on deck, and we're going to have to do whatever it takes to fulfil our promise to Disney, no matter what toll we must pay.

~

'Make it great.'

That had always been Steve Jobs' marching order to John Lasseter. Nothing more, nothing less. But it was still a race to the finish line to get the film done in nine short months. And as *Toy Story 2* co-director Lee Unkrich explained:

> I said, 'Steve, I know we can make a good movie here, but I don't think we can get it out on time. I just don't know how we can do it. It's really intimidating.' And he said to me, 'Lee, you know, when I look back at my career, all of the best work that I've ever done was done under circumstances like this.' Looking back on it, he was absolutely right. *Toy Story 2* is arguably the best film we've made. It fired on all cylinders. But considering the circumstances under which it was made, it makes no sense that it should be as good as it is.[4]

Jobs worked hand-in-hand with Pixar management to ensure both *A Bug's Life* and *Toy Story 2* would be released on time, with the quality for which Pixar was celebrated.

In retrospect, Jobs said the affair was

> a failure of our management. We were not ready to do two things at once. We tried it for all the right reasons, but we failed at it, and we had to go rescue that. It made us even

more cautious in doing that again, and from *Monsters, Inc.* onward it worked great.[5]

RETAIL IS EXPERENTIAL

Before Apple stores dotted the world, retailers treated computers as commodities and displayed them with a warehouse mentality. Because of 'shrinkage' – retailing lingo for shoplifting – computers were bolted down, and peripherals were not hooked up: Look but don't touch, like a toy encased in hard plastic. Understandably, customers were frustrated because they were ready to spend thousands of dollars without the benefit of a hands-on experience. They were expected to buy simply on faith, which doesn't compute.

Compounding the problem were salespeople whose knowledge of Apple products varied widely and whose allegiance was to the manufacturer who paid the best sales incentives, called spiffs. Customers who specifically wanted an Apple computer would often be steered away to a less expensive IBM-compatible. The inevitable result: unhappy customers who soon became disenchanted with computers in general.

'Buying a car is no longer the worst purchasing experience. Buying a computer is now number one,' said Jobs.[6] Unlike cars, there was no way to test-drive a computer in the old days[7] but Jobs wanted to change that. He wanted to engage customers with a memorable in-store experience, which could only be done if Apple controlled the retail experience.

He decided to build a worldwide network of Apple stores, which meant starting from scratch. He would construct a prototype store, solicit feedback and keep iterating until every detail – the layout, the fixtures, the products, the staff, the sales experience – was insanely great. As with everything else at Apple that bore his personal touch, the prototype Apple store, set up in a rented warehouse near Apple's Cupertino campus, was an ongoing work in progress.

Jobs meticulously planned everything that went into the store's appearance and presentation, consuming six months of his time.

The store's layout initially grouped computers by model. It was an easy way to find the desktops in one location, the laptops in another, and so on. Finally, the prototype store in Cupertino was ready for presentation to the Apple board.

But Ron Johnson, the senior vice president of retail operations, had a different, and significantly better, vision: Instead of grouping products together by computers, group them by functional areas. There would be sections for home products, pro products, digital lifestyle solutions, a Genius Bar (to answer questions), a theatre for presentations, software and peripherals.

After all, wasn't that what it was all about? It wasn't about merely displaying computers but interacting with them on a one-to-one basis. People use computers, so why couldn't they experience all of Apple's products in-store the way they were intended? It would closely mimic the customer's in-home experience.

The next day, Johnson presented Jobs with the idea. Jobs exploded. He explained that a lot of work had already gone into the planning phrase, that adopting Johnson's suggestion would mean starting over from scratch. It would mean postponing the public debut of Apple's stores. It would mean more time, money, and effort to reconfigure the stores accordingly.

But there was no denying that Johnson was right. Jobs knew that the best way to enhance the in-store experience at Apple stores was to make it customer-centric.

Jobs went back to the drawing board. Eager Apple customers wanting to visit the finished stores would have to wait just a little longer, but the results would be worth it.

APPLE STORES DEBUT

On 15 May 2001, Apple announced that it would open 25 retail stores across the United States, starting on 19 May with one in Tysons Corner Center mall in Virginia and another in the Glendale Galleria in California.

Steve Jobs explained,

> The Apple stores offer an amazing way to buy a computer. Rather than just hear about megahertz and megabytes, customers can now learn and experience the things they can actually do with a computer, like make movies, burn custom music CDs and publish their digital photos on a personal website.[8]

Not surprisingly, some industry experts proclaimed inevitable failure, notably the president of the research firm Channel Marketing Corp., David A. Goldstein, who said, 'I give them two years before they're turning out the lights on a very painful and expensive mistake.'[9]

Today, at 432 Apple stores in fifteen countries, the lights are still on and shining brightly. Once again, Jobs' critics simply underestimated him.

Now known for their striking design, with spiraling glass staircases that rise skyward, Apple stores are havens for customers who appreciate Apple's superior customer experience.

Learn from your mistakes, and constantly work to improve your life.

17

Invest Time in Your Children

'Once you have a child, your heart is forever outside your body because you are more open and sensitive to things.'

—in *People* magazine, 24 October 2011

LISA: NOT THE COMPUTER

LISA = LOCAL INTEGRATED SYSTEM ARCHItecture. That tortured acronym was the putative name of Apple's new computer designed for the business community, but in fact it was named after Steve Jobs' daughter, Lisa Nicole Brennan, who eventually took her father's name too – Lisa Brennan-Jobs.

Born in 1978 when both of her parents were twenty-three years old, Lisa never benefited from having her father play an active role in her life early on, to the detriment of their relationship. As chronicled in *The Bite in the Apple*, Chrisann Brennan and Steve Jobs had – to put it mildly – a tempestuous relationship that eventually turned into a full-blown war, with Lisa as collateral damage.

Chrisann Brennan lived in one world, and Steve Jobs lived in another. As Lisa explained:

> In California, my mother had raised me mostly alone. We didn't have many things, but she is warm and we were

> happy. We moved a lot. We rented. My father was rich and renowned and later, as I got to know him, went on vacations with him, and then lived with him for a few years, I saw another, more glamorous world. The two sides didn't mix, and I missed one when I had the other.[1]

A Sunday strip for Bill Keane's *The Family Circus* touches on the theme of children and time. One panel shows children being showered by toys, and the next shows them being showered by affection. The message: You can spend money for toys for your children or you can spend time with them; time is better.

In Steve's case, he was there to support Lisa financially – even paying her tuition at Harvard – but he did not have an active physical presence in her life during those critical early years.

Unfortunately, their on-and-off relationship was such that when she graduated from Harvard in 2000, 'She didn't even invite me,' recalled Jobs.[2]

In the last years of his life, Steve urged Lisa to move to California, so they could be closer, but she demurred; she had her own life to live and preferred New York City. Time and circumstance, she felt, made the move impossible. She was a magazine writer who wanted to make her mark, and where else to do so but in the publishing capital of the world? For Lisa, New York City – not California – was the place to be.

Steve Jobs would later regret that he wasn't the father he should and could have been to her, which would have made a positive difference.

But for Jobs, there would be a second act: a set of children with his wife, Laurene.

REED, ERIN AND EVE

Wisdom does not come with age; it comes from learned experience.

The first time around, Steve Jobs was not ready to be a father because he had a lot of growing up to do. The second time around, perhaps somewhat mellowed by his experiences, he was ready.

Children, Jobs said, are 'our hearts running outside our bodies'.[3] And his children so easily tugged at his heartstrings: Reed, who is the mirror image of his father, but with an easy-going nature and gentle ways; Erin, with an artist's sensibilities, who realised how rare her father's time was, because everyone wanted a piece; and Eve, a firecracker whose will is as strong as his own.

After the birth of his children, work was still a big priority in Steve's life – he still had so much he wanted to accomplish at Apple – but he never failed to embrace his three children with Laurene from the beginning, in ways that all parents should.

When Reed was born, [Jobs] began gushing and never stopped. He was a physical dad with each of his children. He fretted over Lisa's boyfriends and Erin's travel and skirt lengths and Eve's safety around the horses she adored,

wrote Mona Simpson.[4]

In a perfect world, Jobs would have lived to see his children graduate from college and sally forth as adults to engage the world and dent the universe, just as he had done.

Jobs did not live in that perfect world. Time was no longer on his side.

Jobs and his family could live anywhere in the world, in a palatial abode if they wished, but instead they lived in Palo Alto, in a residential neighbourhood dotted with other homes that cost in the low millions – not unusual for homes in southern California – and are not ostentatious displays of wealth.

The Jobses wanted their kids to live normal lives, untouched by the 'affluenza' that infected so many rich kids living in southern California.

'His children are the least spoiled people you'll ever meet. They have a graceful reserve,' said a family friend.[5]

> Lack of ostentation was a way of life. No summer homes, no fancy clothes, no chauffeurs or live-in domestic help. Come Halloween, Jobs could be found along the walkway, sometimes in Frankenstein regalia, handing out cartons of organic apple juice and apple-shaped chocolates.[6]

LIKE FATHER, LIKE SON

A picture that ran in the news soon after Steve Jobs died gives one pause. It shows a photo of a well-dressed older man with an iPhone in hand. His uncanny resemblance to Steve Jobs is easily explained: He is Steve Jobs' biological father, Abdulfattah 'John' Jandali.

The two had met when the son was at a San Jose restaurant where the father worked in the mid-eighties. During that chance encounter, neither connected the dots and recognised the strong family resemblance.

When Jandali reached out to his son years later, he was rebuffed. Steve Jobs felt that his father, who contacted him very late in his life, had an ulterior motive. But John Jandali simply wanted to meet the son given up for adoption and sit down to share a cup of coffee because 'just once would make me a very happy man'.[7]

Jandali, who had done well at the Boomtown Casino and didn't need his son's money, gambled by reaching out – keeping in touch, sending simple emails, and, when learning of Jobs' medical condition, sending his medical history with the hope that it would prove useful.

Jandali explained,

> This might sound strange, though, but I am not prepared, even if either of us was on our deathbeds, to pick up the phone and call him. Steve will have to do that, as the Syrian

pride in me does not want him ever to think I am after his fortune.[8]

But Jobs never did that. His biological father waited for a phone call that never came. Steve Jobs, in life, remained apart from his father; now, in death, they would remain apart forever.

When the inevitable news finally came, Jandali, who could not bury his son, instead buried his grief. 'It was not a shock. Basically all you feel is sadness.'[9]

Jandali, a former college professor, now a successful businessman at a Reno casino in Nevada, is a financial success; however, that cannot replace that which is irreplaceable – a few minutes, face to face, with his son with whom, late in life, he so desperately wanted to share a private moment. It is a heartbreaking loss John Jandali will take with him into the next world.

~

It is not the gifts we've received over the years, the technology or other superfluous things, but rather the time we have spent together that we remember and cherish.[10]

—Loreena McKennitt, musician

~

Spend time with your children before it's too late.

THIRD STORY

Death

I never want you to ask what I would have done. Just do what's right.

—Steve Jobs to Tim Cook in 2011

THE BEGINNING AND MIDDLE OF LIFE WAS THE theme for Jobs' first and second stories; the third, on death, explored a dark theme that gives it an unforgettable resonance.

Jobs reminded us that death is 'life's change agent', a natural part of life. We should therefore gracefully accept it and focus on life's journey, not its end.

18

Memento Mori

'… avoid the trap of thinking you have something to lose.'

M*EMENTO MORI* IS LATIN FOR 'REMEMBER that you will die'.

That thought was never far from Steve Jobs' mind. At an early age, he was philosophical by nature, and fixated on the ephemeral nature of time.

In his commencement address, Steve Jobs surprised everyone by ending it with thoughts on his own mortality instead of dispensing traditional optimism. But by talking about his life, and by extension the lives of the Stanford graduates, he makes the point clear: It's later than you think, so get on with your life.

When he was younger, as Jobs told the Stanford graduates, the idea of death was a 'useful but purely intellectual concept'. But as he grew older, the concept turned into an undeniable fact of life: Death is our shared destination, and, as he pointed out to the graduates, it has a purpose in clearing out the old to make room for the new.

Playboy's David Sheff asked Jobs, 'How do you feel about the older companies that have to play catch-up with the younger companies – or perish?'

Jobs replied, 'That's inevitably what happens. That's why I think death is the most wonderful invention of life. It purges the system of these old models that are obsolete.'[1]

Jobs reminds us that we have a narrow window of time to accomplish what we wish to do. The window opens and then closes; that's the nature of life. But at Apple, he lived life to the hilt, to the point where he lived not one but several lifetimes, even before he went on to start his own computer company, NeXT: 'Each year has been so robust with problems and successes and learning experiences and human experiences that a year is a lifetime at Apple. So this has been ten lifetimes,' he told a *Playboy* interviewer.[2]

LIFE'S UNEXPECTED SURPRISES

In 2003, when he was diagnosed with a tumour, the concept of death was not just an abstract thought but a terrifying reality. The prospect gives one pause, and makes one think of life's priorities. In Jobs' case, he made sure a succession plan at Apple was in effect, and worked on projects so that for years to come there would be products that bore his personal imprint. He also spent what time he could with his family, realising that it was a precious commodity dwindling with each passing day.

But even the work and his family took a back seat to treating his illness, which by necessity became the first priority. Jobs held no illusions about his medical condition. Though he downplayed it, the simple truth was that he knew he was fighting for his life. Despite a team of doctors and specialists who tried to keep the cancer at bay with various medical remedies, the effort was like sweeping back the ocean with a broom; eventually he became engulfed.

~

As Jobs stated in his commencement address, there are enormous pressures from other people who, with your best interests at heart, give unsolicited advice on how best to live your life. But what they have lost sight of is that it's *your* life to live, not theirs; this fact also means that *you* must accept responsibility. The only sin, he reminded the graduates, was in living someone *else's* life, and not your own. In his commencement address, Jobs repeated that theme because of its importance.

~

Your life is unique, so live it without regrets because you pass this way only once.

19

Live Life, Accept Death

'If today were the last day of my life ...'

CHRISANN BRENNAN, JOBS' FIRST GIRLFRIEND and Lisa's mother, recalled their many conversations about time passing:

> He told me many times that he would die in his early forties; then one day, when we were in our early forties, he changed the prediction to his mid-forties. When he had become a billionaire but hadn't died by his mid-forties, I remember him repeating, 'I am living on borrowed time,' as if the still-young shaman was angling to carve out a bit more future for himself. [1]

Jobs' acute awareness of time was a key to his productivity. He knew he didn't have time to waste, so he didn't. He instead threw himself into every project, focusing on the end result, and refused to be distracted: He *focused.*

Part of his life's philosophy, drawn from Buddhist teachings, was to simplify all aspects of his life. In terms of his business accomplishments, it meant he focused on the few products he felt were truly transformative; less, he always felt, was more. That's why, when he returned to Apple, he drastically cut product lines across the board. He knew it was better to dazzle customers with brilliant products than baffle them with a confusing selection of too many similar products.

Jobs lived each day accordingly, always looking far down the road to journey's end:

> I think people could choose to do things if they wanted to, but we're all going to be dead soon. That's my point of view. Somebody once told me, 'Live each day as if it would be your last, and one day you'll certainly be right.' I do that. You never know when you're going to go, but you are going to go pretty soon. If you're going to leave anything behind, it's going to be your kids, a few friends, and your work. So that's what I tend to worry about.[2]

ALL WORK

Work formed the largest part of Jobs' life, even at an early age. It was his nature, and he relentlessly drove himself in pursuit of his dreams to create great consumer electronic products.

During his first iteration at Apple, when programmers would work late into the night, they were surprised to see Jobs walking in and out of offices to see what was going on.

During his second iteration at NeXT and Pixar, he again threw himself into his work and recalled how incredibly tired he was when he finally came home at the end of a long workday.

The third iteration came when he triumphantly returned to Apple as CEO and, in quick succession, brought out one amazing product after another: the iPod in 2001, the iPhone in 2007 and the iPad in 2010. Bringing Apple back to its former glory was, he found, a daunting challenge.

ONLY TIME

By that time, he was married and had three children with his wife, Laurene, plus one from a former relationship, and he was stretched too thin, which took a drastic toll on the time he could spend with his family. They had to be satisfied with what they got, not what they wanted.

The time equation was further complicated by an overriding demon that trumped everything – his failing health, which toward the end was so debilitating that he could only look at, but not eat, specially prepared sushi and soba, which he loved.

Though he was able to hide the severity of his illness from his own employees, Jobs could not expect the media to afford him the same respect. Specifically, in a piece for *The New York Times*, Joe Nocera complained about Jobs' lack of transparency on health issues.

Nocera soon received an unexpected phone call: Jobs himself called to give him a taste of his own medicine. 'This is Steve Jobs. You think I'm an arrogant **** who thinks he's above the law, and I think you're a slime bucket who gets most of his facts wrong.'[3]

The facts: Jobs got a life-saving liver transplant in 2009, in Tennessee. But by late 2010, his weight dropped so drastically that he could no longer sugarcoat the truth. One look at him and anyone could see his health was steadily deteriorating. And by the summer of 2011, he knew it was time to pass the baton to Tim Cook, the chief operating officer whom he had been grooming for the CEO position.

It was now Cook's responsibility to see that Apple's projects reached fruition.

~

In a rare interview given by Steve Jobs' daughter Erin in the year her father died, she shed light on just how the scarcity of his time had an impact on her life. As Erin told her father's official biographer, she dealt with his absence philosophically.

> Sometimes I wish I had more of his attention, but I know the work he's doing is very important and I think it's really cool, so I'm fine. I don't really need more attention.[4]

She didn't *need* more of his attention, but, like any daughter, she would gladly have accepted it. Resigned to the inevitable, she gracefully accepted what she could get. So, too, did her father, who loved his work and his family with the certain knowledge that he was indeed living on borrowed time, just as he had foreseen back when he was in his early twenties.

But at my back I always hear
Time's winged chariot hurrying near.
—Andrew Marvell, 'To His Coy Mistress'

Time is priceless because it cannot be replaced. So strive to live each day to your fullest potential.

20

Deal with the Reality of the Situation

'I lived with that [cancer] diagnosis all day.'

CANCER.

It's a terrifying word that can cause people to react in horror, shock, disbelief or anger. It's a sobering reminder that life really is too short – and for those so diagnosed, even shorter.

In October 2003, a test showed that Steve Jobs had a pancreatic neuroendocrine tumour. That was the bad news. The good news was that because the doctors had caught it early on, there was a chance to treat it before it spread throughout his body. But it would require immediate surgery.

Faced with those facts, most people would quickly opt for surgery; and the sooner, the better, because once cancer starts spreading, it is increasingly more difficult to treat.

In Jobs' case, he decided not to have the immediate surgery; worse, nobody – not his wife, not his trusted friends, not the team of doctors – could change his mind.

Jobs then embarked on a self-directed course to heal himself by various means, when only immediate surgery would have made a difference.

Jobs, as he had done in the past, ignored the reality of the situation. But it was a risk he chose to take, and it was his call to make. After all, invasive surgery is never anyone's first choice, but when it's your *only* choice, your only real hope, you take a deep breath and put your faith in your team of doctors and let them do their jobs.

When Jobs' self-directed course proved ineffective, it became apparent to him that he no longer had a choice in the matter, if he wanted to live. He elected to have surgery at nearby Stanford University Medical Center.

On 31 July 2004, Jobs underwent surgery to remove the tumour in an operation called a pancreatoduodenectomy. 'The surgery removes the right side of the pancreas, the gallbladder, and parts of the stomach, bile duct and small intestine.'[1] The doctors had hoped that would be sufficient, but when the cancer had spread to the liver, Jobs had no choice but to have a second operation – this time, a liver transplant.

He was put on a waiting list at Methodist University Hospital in Memphis, when it became clear that being on a waiting list in California would not be timely. On the weekend of 21 March 2009, Jobs flew in his personal jet to Memphis, where he had the operation. He returned to California in May 2009.

TURNING FIFTY

Forty, not fifty, years old is the midpoint of a human life.

On 24 February 2005, Jobs celebrated his fiftieth birthday and, in light of his medical condition, was in a reflective, albeit somber, mood.

When Stanford University asked him to deliver a commencement address at its June 2005 graduation ceremony, Jobs agreed. He had personal things on his mind that he wanted to say in a public forum, which was rare for him. He routinely discussed business matters at Apple product events or during interviews, but he held personal matters close to his heart and rarely discussed them.

Though Jobs had never given a commencement address before, it seemed logical that he'd give his first, and only, address to Stanford, which had special meaning for him. It was there that he had met with a biochemist named Paul Berg who was the catalyst for NeXT, which Jobs started after leaving Apple. Moreover, the school's ties to Silicon Valley were extensive and far-reaching, and Apple had its fair share of Stanford graduates. Jobs also loved to walk around its campus, twenty-one kilometres from Apple's, where he could clear his mind and think creatively. And it was at a lecture at Stanford that he met his wife, Laurene Powell.

Jobs decided to use this rare opportunity to share his life's story and lessons learned. He would speak from the heart. The graduates had no idea they'd be watching him deliver the most popular and most-watched commencement address in history.

THE UNKNOWABLE QUESTION

If Jobs had heeded the doctors' urgent recommendation to have surgery to remove the tumour when it was first detected, would he still be alive today? Or, perhaps, would he have lived longer?

We don't know. We *can't* know. But what we *do* know is that at a critical juncture in his life, Steve Jobs postponed a decision regarding surgery, despite his doctors' insistence. But by then it was too late, and Jobs lived to regret it.

For of all sad words of tongue or pen,
the saddest are these: 'It might have been ...'

—John Greenleaf Whittier, *Maud Miller*

The reality of the situation never changes; you can only change your perception of it. Consider all the facts and then choose wisely.

21

Embrace Idealism

'Don't be trapped by dogma.'

WHOLE EARTH CATALOG

STEVE JOBS TOLD STANFORD GRADUATES THAT the *Whole Earth Catalog* had been like a bible for his generation. First published in 1968 in catalogue form, its subtitle was 'access to tools'. It was, as Jobs told them, 'sort of like Google in paperback form'. It also predated Google by thirty-five years.

The catalogue inspired Jobs because of its idealism and its fundamental belief that ordinary people should have access to tools. Stewart Brand, the catalogue's founder, realised the times they were a-changing and

> a realm of intimate, personal power is developing – power of the individual to conduct his own education, find his own inspiration, shape his own environment, and share his adventure with whoever is interested.[1]

CUT-AND-PASTE BY HAND

Back then, putting together such a catalogue was no easy task. It was a labour of love. In the pre-Mac days, phototypesetting required hiring a production house to input text, print it out on long sheets of photo-sensitive paper, and cut pieces to paste them in place. It was tedious work, expensive and prone to error.

A TYPEWRITER WITH 'GOLF' BALLS

Stewart Brand's brilliant flash of insight was to set type by using a special typewriter: the IBM Selectric Composer, which had interchangeable 'golf balls', each with a different font. The $6,000 typewriter gave Brand's staff the ability to set type on the spot, make changes as necessary, and without the prohibitive expense of phototypesetting. The process, though, was no less tedious.

Firmly rooted in the turbulent 1960s, at a time when young Americans took to the streets to rebel against big government and big business, the *Catalog* was mind-expanding in a constructive way: It provided knowledge, and by doing so gave power to the people. It would change the world one person at a time. It was idealistic. It fit the ethos of that time: Empower the individual.

In its oversized pages, the *Whole Earth Catalog* filtered the wheat from the chaff. It recommended products (mostly books) according to strict criteria: As the catalogue stated, the product had to be 'useful as a tool, relevant to independent education, high quality or low cost, not already common knowledge, and easily available by mail'.

> I want to make this thing called a 'whole Earth' catalog so that anyone on Earth can pick up a telephone and find out the complete information on anything ... That's my goal,
>
> recalled Stewart Brand.[2]

~

THE MACINTOSH: A COMPUTER FOR THE REST OF US

Jobs told Stanford graduates that the *Whole Earth Catalog* was 'idealistic, and overflowing with neat tools and great notions'. And with that firmly in mind, he too wanted to change the world – but do it his way. His tool would be an easy-to-use personal computer, a more powerful fulcrum.

Jobs knew that many people simply saw no immediate need for a home computer. As he told *Playboy*, 'The hard part of what we're up against now is that people ask you about specifics and you can't tell them.'[3] Before the Apple II and the Mac, computers were more suited for small offices and businesses instead of individuals, because of the costs involved in buying the computer and all the peripherals necessary to make it useful.

Moreover, the primitive personal computers of that time meant mastering software, which was an education in itself.

The Apple II was a good start but a long way from Jobs' vision of the ideal computer for the rest of us.

It was, Jobs knew, time for a fundamental change, and nobody else in the industry was exploring the uncharted territory.

The computer itself would have to be simplified, to the point where you could take it out of a box, plug it in, turn it on and begin using it. In other words, it had to be as easy to use as an appliance or a bike, which was Jobs' metaphor for the Mac.

Jobs' inspiration was to make a computer that would be that easy for people. Only then would people embrace it; only then would people bring it into their homes and use it to change their lives.

While other computer manufacturers were happy to commoditise their computers with little regard to the consumer experience, which meant users were often frustrated and gave up on computers altogether, Steve Jobs' vision of simplicity struck a responsive chord: The Mac wouldn't intimidate the user – it would *inspire* the user.

Just as the *Whole Earth Catalog* was an ideal tool for its time, so was the Mac, which gave everybody (in the words of an Apple advertising slogan) 'the power to be your best'.

~

Jobs' critics viewed him as a modern-day savior whose 'software evangelists' (as Jobs termed them) were sent forth to spread his gospel. But a more apt comparison would be Prometheus, who gave the gift of fire to mankind by stealing it from the god Zeus.

Computing power, once the exclusive domain of big businesses that could afford to lease expensive mainframe computers, was now available in an intuitively designed desktop computer that brought its power to everyone at a click of the mouse. Jobs saw the Macintosh as the ultimate tool to harness that power:

> I think one of the things that really separates us from the high primates is that we're tool builders. I read a study that measured the efficiency of locomotion for various species on the planet. The condor used the least energy to move a kilometre. And humans came in with a rather unimpressive showing, about a third of the way down the list. It was not too proud a showing for the crown of creation. So, that didn't look so good. But then somebody at *Scientific American* had the insight to test the efficiency of locomotion for a man on a bicycle. And, a man on a bicycle, a human on a bicycle, blew the condor away, completely off the top of the charts.
>
> And that's what a computer is to me ... the most remarkable tool that we've ever come up with, and it's the equivalent of a bicycle for our minds. [4]

Jobs loved the idea that the Mac was the first truly intuitive home computer to open up a world of possibilities for the user, including desktop publishing. The Mac recalled the *Whole Earth Catalog.*

Eventually all computers, including the Mac, would be even more powerful tools empowering the individual because of access to the World Wide Web. Back in the day, when the Mac was new, the web was in its infancy. No one – including Steve Jobs – knew precisely how it would change our lives. As Jobs said in 1997: 'The internet is certainly doing it on a larger scale than some people had imagined. But what this all means yet I don't know.'[5]

Back in 1996–1997, the web was accessed principally by a thousand universities and laboratories. Today, the web hosts 634 million websites, with 3 billion search queries daily and serves 2.7 billion users worldwide (39 per cent of the world's population).

The web transformed the world into a global electronic village, accessible by smartphones that have democratised access to information: from the world's most populous cities to small villages in Africa, the smartphone is omnipresent.

YOU SAY YOU WANT A REVOLUTION …

Stewart Brand's generation was the age of typewriters and fixed print, but Steve Jobs' generation was the age of personal computers and electronic print. Both were fuelled by idealism, by the idea that information was power and that access to that power belonged not to the rich or the powerful but to all of us … and thereby began a revolution with computers that empowered the individual.

As Walt Disney liked to say about his company, 'I only hope we don't lose sight of one thing – that it was all started by a mouse.'[6]

The same could be said of the tale of Apple's Macintosh.

~

Embrace idealism – empower your vision and ideas.

22

Stay Hungry. Stay Foolish.

'... have the courage to follow your heart and intuition.'

STAY HUNGRY

The image I had in my mind was that of a hitchhiker at dawn on a road somewhere and the sun comes up and there are trains going by. The frame of mind of the young hitchhiker is one of the freest frames of mind there is. You're always a little bit hungry and you know you are being completely foolish.

—Stewart Brand[1]

WHEN STEVE JOBS TOLD STANFORD GRADuates that to stay hungry was what he 'always wished … for myself' and for them, too, he wasn't speaking literally; he wasn't wishing they all would miss meals.

Ironically, when he was in college, Jobs stayed perpetually hungry because there was no money for food. He collected soda bottles from roadsides for their five-cent deposits, earning enough money to buy his next meal, mostly cereal. As he told the Stanford students, he was so poor that he ate only one substantial meal during the week, which involved an eleven-kilometre trek from campus to the nearest Hare Krishna temple. It was a free meal called the Sunday Love Feast.

Jobs' reference to 'staying hungry' was more an expression of a desire for knowledge, for enlightenment, than a hunger for success in an increasingly materialistic world.

Jobs, who was mostly a vegetarian, lived as simple an existence as possible. When he was a freshman in college, he had no car, no money, no fancy clothes – none of the trappings of traditional success – and he didn't care; moreover, he didn't care what people thought of him either. A hippie in spirit and appearance, he rejected excessive materialism. And he loved his simple life. As Jobs explained:

> What is a hippie? … [It's] beyond what you see every day. Beyond a job, two cars in the garage, and a career. There's something more that's going on. There's another side of the coin that we don't talk about much, and we experience it when there's gaps, when everything is not ordered and perfect.[2]

Jobs rented an unheated garage apartment, despite western Oregon's cool temperatures, for $20 a month; he supplemented his bare-bones living by working at Reed College's psychology lab, where he tended to the electronic equipment.

Jobs eked out a subsistence living during the time he was at Reed College, but he didn't care. What he didn't want was to be caught up and trapped by material possessions in a rat race like some of his contemporaries. Jobs wasn't going to climb the ladder of success by starting at the bottom, playing office politics, and working himself up from rung to rung, until he reached the top three decades later. He'd instead reach the top by faster means: He'd start his own technology company.

THE OUTLIER

After leaving Reed College, he headed home and worked briefly for Nolan Bushnell at the gaming company Atari. Bushnell recalled that Jobs 'was very often the smartest guy in the room, and he would let people know that'.[3] Still, Jobs was never going to be the model employee. He bathed infrequently, smelled bad, and took to relieving his stress by putting his bare feet in a toilet – a poor man's Jacuzzi.

But none of that mattered to Bushnell. He saw beneath Jobs' hippie facade to see the creative talent hidden within. Bushnell recalled, 'He acted. In fact, he never stopped acting. He was constantly tackling new ideas, putting new concepts into play, looking for the next big thing.'[4]

TRANSCENDENCE IN INDIA

After leaving Atari, Jobs and a college friend, Daniel Kotte, went to India. They were inspired by a book they discovered at Reed College titled *Be Here Now* by Ram Dass.

After reading the book, Jobs and Kotte took Dass's words to heart; they felt it important to go to India and seek enlightenment, and return home as enlightened souls. As pilgrims, they would seek the ashram of Indian guru Neem Karoli Baba, but when they eventually reached it, they found it deserted because he had died. It was one of the many rude awakenings they experienced in India, a culture with grinding poverty that contrasted sharply to the modern conveniences of the Western world to which Jobs was accustomed and took for granted.

What Jobs and Kotte took from their sojourn in India included hunger, dysentery, more hunger, an encounter with a lynch mob that ran them out of town, theft of traveller's cheques, and a flash flood so severe that they prayed to God to save them from drowning.

When asked how Steve Jobs was influenced by the experience, Kotte spoke for both of them when he replied:

> I think the trip influenced us both in a general sense of broadening our experience of life on earth and putting our lives in the U.S. in a wider perspective. Neither of us found a 'guru' or had a 'miracle story' or an encounter with someone with advanced yogic powers, but I would say that wasn't particularly a disappointment … I think what stayed with both of us was an appreciation for the rich culture of India and the huge contrast between opulence and poverty to be found there.[5]

Jobs also took away from his Indian experience an awareness of the fundamental difference between Eastern and Western thinking. Jobs' celebration of Eastern spirituality is at the cornerstone of how he envisioned products, according to Brett Robinson, who wrote *Appletopia:*

> Steve Jobs felt his experience in India had a major impact on his work. The power of intuition captivated him, so much so that it became the hallmark of his product design and philosophy. He found the most striking examples of intuitive thought and experiential wisdom among the illiterate Hindu villagers who served as hosts and guides on his journey. It became clear to Jobs that his calling was to develop tools for the mind that would deprogram the Western mentality of linear rationality and formal logic.[6]

STAY FOOLISH

'Stay foolish', the second part of Brand's admonition that Jobs embraced, refers to a state of mind – one as free as possible, without constraints, as Brand explained: an unburdened mind, capable of thinking clearly and creatively; in short, a free thinker, someone who has 'rejected authority and dogma, especially in religious thinking, in favour of rational inquiry and speculation'.[7] Or in Apple's terms, someone who would 'think different', the theme of an Apple ad highlighting artists like Picasso, John Lennon, Bob Dylan and others.

ON THE ROAD AGAIN

For Jobs, the *journey* was the reward; and the metaphor of the open road, with all that it promised, was critical to how Jobs thought: He dropped into college – and dropped out; he took recreational drugs – and experienced a wheat field playing Bach music; he went to India – and returned with a new way of thinking; and he went, time and again, to Kyoto in Japan – and found simplicity, which he incorporated into all his products.

THE COMPASSED HEART

Jobs wished that the Stanford graduates, like him, would become pilgrims who set out on a path with a clear and open mind to discover that life should be an adventure; a life not mapped out by others who are going to tell you what to do and where to go; instead, he told us, trust your heart.

Follow the open road, and follow your heart. It will show you the way.

One More Thing

… Letting Go

'You never know when you're going to go, but you are going to go pretty soon. If you're going to leave anything behind, it's going to be your kids, a few friends, and your work.'

—in Oral History Interview,
Smithsonian Institution, 1995

WHEN APPLE INCORPORATED ON 1 APRIL 1976, the company had three co-founders. Two of them, obviously, are well known in retrospect and synonymous with Apple: the two Steves – Jobs and Wozniak. But the third remained largely unknown and in truth is a minor footnote in Apple's history: Ronald Wayne, who got cold feet and bailed out after eleven days. (Had he retained his 10 per cent share of Apple stock, he would be a billionaire today.)

Wozniak also left early on, in 1985; he returned in 1997 as an unpaid advisor to Apple's then-CEO, Gil Amelio. But only Steve Jobs was in for the long haul. He stayed for a total of twenty-three years (1976–1985, 1997–2011), and hoped to be at Apple's helm for decades to come.[1] But that was not to be.

When it was time to step down, he drafted a letter and revised it until he boiled it down to its essence in five concise paragraphs. He addressed it to the Apple board of directors and the Apple community. Despite his failing health, he wanted to deliver the letter in person, though that was not necessary: He could have simply mailed it, faxed it or had it hand-delivered.

But he chose to hand-deliver it himself at a board meeting held on Apple's campus in Cupertino on 24 August 2011.

Because his health did not permit him to walk under his own power, Jobs arrived in a wheelchair and went directly to the boardroom, where Apple's directors and first-echelon managers sat around a large table.

Uncharacteristically quiet, rail thin and obviously weak, Jobs told the board he had something he wanted to share with them alone. The room was cleared so that only the six directors remained.

Jobs read them the entire letter, which began:

> *I have always said if there ever came a day when I could no longer meet my duties and expectations as Apple's CEO, I would be the first to let you know. Unfortunately, that day has come.*
>
> *I hereby resign as CEO of Apple. I would like to serve, if the Board sees fit, as Chairman of the Board, director and Apple employee.*

He signed it simply 'Steve'.

~

At that point, he only had forty-three more days to live.

He had hoped to serve as Apple's board chairman, but it was a false hope. But his letter made the point that, ill as he was, he wanted to contribute to Apple to the very end of his days.

He was Apple to the core.

Steve Jobs' world shrank in geographic size. He could no longer walk the grounds of his beloved 850,000-square-foot Apple Campus. Jobs was now bedridden at home in a downstairs bedroom because he could no longer manage the stairs. He spent most of his time watching TV.

In *The New York Times*, Steve's sister, Mona Simpson, recalled:

> He told me, when he was saying goodbye and telling me he was sorry, so sorry we wouldn't be able to be old together as we'd always planned, that he was going to a better place.

On 5 October 2011, Steven Paul Jobs' journey ended. He went gently into that good night.

LOVE IS ALL YOU NEED

After Jobs' death, the home page for Apple's website displayed a black-and-white photo of Jobs. Taken by Albert Watson, it is a powerful portrait of him in his prime, the way he'd want to be remembered: a figure of strength with an intense look, piercing eyes, and utterly confident and self-assured. (The photograph appeared a month later as the book cover to *Steve Jobs*, his official biography, written by Walter Isaacson.) The text read: 'Steve Jobs 1955–2011.'

Jobs would have approved. It was simple, elegant and understated.

A Californian by birth and an American by citizenship, Steve Jobs was clearly a citizen of the world at large, judged by the spontaneous public outpouring of love from Apple fans and prominent figures, who bowed their heads to a man who changed our world one Mac, one iPod, one iPhone and one iPad at a time.

At Apple stores worldwide, fans lit candles and left condolence notes, bouquets of fragrant flowers, countless photographs of Jobs and large posters bearing his photograph.

And enough apples to fill orchards.

In a private ceremony, Steve Jobs was buried at the Alta Mesa Memorial Park in Palo Alto, California, where his adoptive parents, Paul and Clara Jobs, were also buried.

Fittingly, another major tech figure, David Packard, co-founder of Hewlett-Packard, is also there. And – you gotta love it, because Jobs loved rock 'n' roll – so is Ron 'Pigpen' McKernan, a founding band member of the Grateful Dead.

By design, Jobs' gravesite is unmarked. There is no headstone, no figurine of a winged angel overlooking his plot. In death, as in life, simplicity was Jobs' order of the day. *Don't dwell on me,* he constantly reminded us. *Pay attention, instead, to the things of beauty I created. The insanely great products. That's what my life's work was all about. Now go and find your life's passion and make your own dent in the universe.*

Apple co-founder Steve 'Woz' Wozniak

We've lost something we won't get back. The way I see it, though, the way people love products he put so much into creating means he brought a lot of life to the world.[2]

Apple CEO Tim Cook

I have some very sad news to share with all of you. Steve passed away earlier today.

Apple has lost a visionary and creative genius, and the world has lost an amazing human being. Those of us who have been fortunate enough to know and work with Steve have lost a dear friend and an inspiring mentor. Steve leaves behind a company that only he could have built, and his spirit will forever be the foundation of Apple.[3]

Pixar's John Lasseter and Ed Catmull

Steve Jobs was an extraordinary visionary, our very dear friend and the guiding light of the Pixar family. He saw the potential of what Pixar could be before the rest of us, and beyond what anyone ever imagined. Steve took a chance on us and believed in our crazy dream of making computer animated films; the one thing he always said was to simply 'make it great'.[4]

President Barack Obama

By building one of the planet's most successful companies from his garage, he exemplified the spirit of American ingenuity. By making computers personal and putting the internet in our pockets, he made the information revolution not only accessible, but intuitive and fun. And by turning his talents to storytelling, he has brought joy to millions of children and grown-ups alike. Steve was fond of saying that he lived every day like it was his last. Because he did, he transformed our lives, redefined entire industries, and achieved one of the rarest feats in human history: he changed the way each of us sees the world.[5]

Former Microsoft founder William 'Bill' Gates III

I'm truly saddened to learn of Steve Jobs' death. Melinda and I extend our sincere condolences to his family and friends, and to everyone Steve has touched through his work.

... The world rarely sees someone who has had the profound impact Steve has had, the effects of which will be felt for many generations to come.[6]

Sir Paul McCartney

I once said to him that he must be extremely proud of what he had done. He agreed but said he was even prouder of what he had not done. A great man who will be missed by me and many others.[7]

In the U.S., Post-it notes were affixed to Apple's storefront windows: *RIP to an Innovator … 'Stay Hungry, Stay Foolish' … Steve Great Jobs … A life well-lived … We love you … Artist, Creator, Genius, You Changed the World … Insanely Grateful … Thank you for caring about the big picture and the smallest detail … iSad.*

And on countless notes, just a simple, hand-drawn symbol – the human heart.

> *OH WOW. OH WOW. OH WOW.*
>
> —Steve Jobs' sister Mona Simpson,
> recalling his last words

> ***Our birth is but a sleep and a forgetting:***
> ***The Soul that rises with us, our life's Star,***
> ***Hath had elsewhere its setting,***
> ***And cometh from afar.***
>
> —William Wordsworth (1770–1850),
> 'Ode: Intimations of Immortality
> from Recollections of Childhood'

Connecting the Dots in Steve Jobs' Life

BOOKS: PAPERBACK WRITER

As Jobs told *The New York Times* in January 2008,

> It doesn't matter how good or bad the product is, the fact is that people don't read anymore. Forty per cent of the people in the U.S. read one book or less last year. The whole conception is flawed at the top because people don't read anymore.[1]

Or so he'd have people believe. Jobs knew that people read books, in print and e-book form. In truth, he was throwing sand in everyone's eyes because Apple was developing its own proprietary e-books for its iPad, which he released three years later.

Jobs loved books. As he told *Playboy*, 'Well, my favourite things in life are books, sushi …'[2] A photo taken in 2004 by Diana Walker depicts his home office with three bookshelves crammed with books. What we don't know is how many other books he had in his collection. But we can see his curiosity encompassed a broad range of subject matter: According to Walter Isaacson, Jobs' book collection included diet books, self-help books about Eastern philosophy, classic literature, poetry, and Clayton Christensen's formative book, *The Innovator's Dilemma.*

Jobs considered books to be tools, which is not surprising: He was a big fan of the *Whole Earth Catalog*, which held books in the same regard.

CLOTHES MAKE THE MAN

At Reed College, Jobs dressed like a bohemian, inspired by the hippies of the 1960s. He went barefoot, unless it snowed, which necessitated footwear – sandals.

He left college to move back home and work full time at Atari, where he stood out: Because he bathed infrequently and never used deodorant, he stank, resulting in complaints from engineers who didn't want to work with him. Atari's Nolan Bushnell recalled that because both Jobs and Wozniak preferred to work late into the night, the company accommodated them.

> Soon the Steves brought in futons and stored them under their desks so they could work until 3 a.m. and then catch five or six hours of sleep. There wasn't any place to shower or bathe.[3]

Leaving Atari permanently behind, he headed to India. He gave away or sold his Western clothes and reportedly adopted the traditional pilgrim's loincloth.

In his early years at Apple Computer, he wore three-piece suits as befitting his role as a sales and marketing executive. He wore his hair long and sported a mustache and a beard.

By the early 1980s, leading up to the release of the Macintosh in 1984, Jobs dressed immaculately in tailored suits and conservative long-sleeve shirts. (At that time, John Molloy's guidebook for corporate dress, *Dress for Success*, was popular.) Jobs also adopted a clean-shaven look: no more mustache, beard and longer hair. The conservative look was what Wall Street and the business community expected to see, and Jobs delivered.

At NeXT, he dressed down for day-to-day work but dressed up in a business suit for sales purposes.

At Pixar, he dressed informally and casually, which was consistent with the corporate culture.

When he returned to Apple in 1997, he dispensed with the traditional corporate uniform of suit-and-tie, and replaced it with black turtleneck sweaters, Levi's 501 jeans without a belt, and New Balance 900-series sneakers, which he had been wearing for some years. It became his trademark look: Zen-like in its elegance and simplicity, it was functional and made a personal statement: I'll dress to suit myself. It is the look most people now identify with Jobs.

THE SOUND OF MUSIC

When Steve Jobs finally met one of his musical idols, Bob Dylan, the normally articulate Apple co-founder found himself tongue-tied, to Dylan's amusement. Early on, Jobs was exposed to Dylan's music and, with Steve Wozniak, compared it to that of the Beatles, to decide whom they favoured. As Woz recalled in his autobiography,

> We both favoured Dylan because the songs were about life and living and the values in life and what was really important … The songs the Beatles did were not as deep down and affecting your soul and emotions as Dylan's were. They were more like pop songs. To us, Dylan's songs struck a moral chord. They kind of made you think about what was right and wrong in the world and how you're going to live and be.[4]

Let It Be

Exposed to Beatles music early in his life – he was only nine when the Beatles invaded America on 7 February 1964 – Jobs, like so many others, got caught up in Beatlemania. Even more than Dylan, the Beatles provided the soundtrack to Jobs' life.

Years later, when he created iTunes, his major goal was to get the Beatles' library available digitally, by song or by album, which had never been done. One of his proudest moments was finally achieving that goal in November 2010:

'We're really excited to bring the Beatles' music to iTunes,' said Sir Paul McCartney. 'It's fantastic to see the songs we originally released on vinyl receive as much love in the digital world as they did the first time around.'

'I am particularly glad to no longer be asked when the Beatles are coming to iTunes,' said Ringo Starr. 'At last, if you want it – you can get it now – The Beatles from Liverpool to now! Peace and Love, Ringo.'

'In the joyful spirit of "Give Peace a Chance", I think it is so appropriate that we are doing this on John's 70th birthday year,' said Yoko Ono Lennon.

'The Beatles on iTunes – Bravo!' said Olivia Harrison.

'We love the Beatles and are honoured and thrilled to welcome them to iTunes,' said Steve Jobs.

> It has been a long and winding road to get here. Thanks to the Beatles and EMI, we are now realising a dream we've had since we launched iTunes ten years ago.[5]

A barefoot hippie who became a billionaire businessman, Jobs took his music seriously, investing thousands of dollars in separate components in his search for sonic purity. In a photo taken in 1982 by Diana Walker, Jobs is seated on the floor of a bare living room; behind him, a towering pair of electrostatic 3 speakers bracketing separate components: a Threshold FET preamplifier, a Michell Gyro turntable, and a Denon TU-750S tuner.

It was the same year that Mobile Fidelity Sound Lab issued an audiophile vinyl box of *The Beatles: The Collection*, which Jobs loved so much that he bought two sets: one for himself and one for Hartmut Esslinger (the company founder of Frog Design), because when they worked together, they had to listen to music they could mutually agree on, and their common choice was the Beatles: '[W]e played Beatles LPs non-stop during our creative discussions and while we were sketching, cutting quick models and fantasising about global success.'[6]

Walkman

Years later, in 1985, when Steve Jobs and John Sculley visited Sony chairman Akio Morita at one of his factories, they received free Sony Walkmans, then state of the art, which played compact discs.

Jobs promptly took his apart to see what made it tick.

Jobs' great love of music was instrumental in developing the iTunes Store. The iPod was a giant leap forward over the existing MP3 players at the time.

Music for Memorial Service

Just as music spoke to him when he was a teenager, things came full circle when, at Stanford University's Memorial Church, the sound of sweet music filled the air at his memorial service: Joan Baez, whom he dated briefly, sang 'Swing Low, Sweet Chariot'. Bono sang one of Jobs' favourite Bob Dylan songs, 'Every Grain of Sand'. And cellist Yo-Yo Ma, whose music made Jobs shed tears because he considered it sublime, played a Bach suite.

OBJECTS OF ART

Jobs was not a traditional consumer, furnishing every room in a house. But when he saw something he considered exquisite, he bought it because of its beauty, and not the investment potential. As it turned out, many of his hand-picked possessions proved to be good investments. Some prominent examples come to mind.

Tiffany Floor Lamp

In the aforementioned photograph by Diana Walker, a floor lamp provides the sole illumination in his living room. It is no ordinary lamp; it's an original Tiffany lamp circa 1910. A comparable lamp sold at auction in the early 1980s for $120,000.

The same lamp today would fetch up to $200,000, according to a Christie's auction of a private collection in 2013.[7]

Ansel Adams Photographs

Today's digital generation views original photographic prints in the same light as they do vinyl records and compact discs – they see them as historical artefacts of a bygone era. But for most of the history of photography, when companies like Kodak dominated the market, there was an art to making one-of-a-kind prints in a darkroom using trays of chemicals.

Adams' black-and-white photographs, taken with large-format view cameras, have a tonal range unmatched by digital prints. He developed a tonal 'Zone System' inspired by his training as a classical pianist. By 'playing' with the light, he was able to dramatically emphasise what he considered the most important photographic value in a print.

Best known for his landscapes from Yosemite National Park, Adams was equally skilled at industrial photography, portraits and other subjects.

Steve Jobs collected Adams' work with a passion. Adams' prices have, over the years, steadily risen. His best-known photograph (*Moonrise over Hernandez County*) sold in 2006 for $609,600 at Sotheby's New York.

Among the original prints owned by Jobs is a 1944 photograph titled *Winter Sunrise, Sierra Nevada from Lone Pine.* Previously owned by Adams' daughter, Ann Adams Helms, the mural-size print is worth a fortune. A small print of that image sold at auction at Phillips in New York City in 2011 for $43,750.

Expensive Toys for Boys

BMW R 60/2 motorcycle (1966 model). Jobs was a big fan of German engineering, so it's no wonder that, when he wanted a bike, he passed on Japanese bikes and went for a classic from Bavarian Motor Works (BMW). Designed as a touring motorcycle for long hauls, with a 600 cc engine, the machine had a top speed of 145 kilometres per hour.

Mercedes SL 55 AMG (2008 model). Originally costing $130,175, this high-performance car had a supercharged V8 engine.

Jobs reportedly leased a new car every six months, which allowed him to use a loophole in California law: A new car must have a plate affixed no later than six months. So he drove without plates simply by switching cars.

Yacht *Venus.* Designed by Phillipe Starck, this 256-footer was commissioned by Jobs in 2007 for $138 million. The oceangoing vessel launched from the Feadship shipyards in Aalsmeer, the Netherlands, on 28 October 2012 – a year after Jobs died.

The yacht's name is a reference to the Roman goddess famous for love, beauty, sex, fertility, and prosperity. It also recalls the famous Botticelli painting, *The Birth of Venus*, which shows a nude goddess demurely covering herself as she stands on top of a large half-shell.

Learjet (Gulfstream GLF5). A long-range business jet that Jobs got as a gift from the Apple board in 2000: When asked by the Apple board members how they could show their appreciation for saving the company, Jobs requested a jet because, with his growing family, he found it increasingly frustrating to travel on commercial airlines.

Ed Woolard, an Apple board member, explained the $90 million cost (plane plus sales and income taxes):

> Apple's market [capitalisation] has risen from less than $2 billion to over $16 billion under Steve's leadership since his return to the company two and a half years ago. Steve has taken no compensation thus far, and we are therefore delighted to give him this airplane in appreciation of the great job he has done for our shareholders during this period.[8]

Jobs used the jet most often to take his family to one of his favourite destinations – Kona, Hawaii – that he and his wife visited every spring for more than two decades, according to journalist Betsy Morris.[9]

Designers

Jobs, who had no formal training in design, had an intuitive feel for it. His work with some of the best artists and graphic designers of our time helped give Jobs' products their distinctive design.

Jean-Michel Folon, a French artist who died in 2005, was commissioned to design 'Mister Macintosh'. Jobs said:

> Mr Macintosh is a mysterious little man who lives inside each Macintosh. He pops up every once in a while, when you least expect it, and then winks at you and disappears again. It will be so quick that you won't be sure if you saw him or not. We'll plant references in the manuals to the legend of Mr Macintosh, and no one will know if he's real or not.[10]

His whimsical design was not practical, though: His bitmapped images took up too much storage space. So Mr Macintosh exists only on some pins given out to the Mac team and etched on the logic boards of early production models of the Mac.

Folon also accepted a commission to draw a logo that would appear when the Macintosh started up. The $30,000 logo showed a flying man with a Mac computer for a head, holding a keyboard under one arm. Moreover, Folon had negotiated a royalty of $1 for every Mac sold, which would have earned him $30 million. But 'The Macintosh Spirit' design never took flight. Instead, Jobs decided not to use the art and had the logo drawn in-house.

Folon's third commission, depicting a man on a bike with a Mac behind the seat, was used for the 'Wheels for the Mind' educational initiative. (Its inspiration was Jobs' oft-stated idea that a computer was a bicycle for the mind.)

Paul Rand accepted a commission to design a logo from Jobs for $100,000. He delivered an eye-catching logo, a black cube with coloured letters, accompanied by a 100-page booklet to explain its design.

The job was a take-it-or-leave-it commission. Jobs explained,

> I asked him if he would come up with a few options, and he said, 'No, I will solve your problem for you and you will pay me. You don't have to use the solution. If you want options go talk to other people.'[11]

When Jobs saw the final artwork, he wanted a minor change to the colour of one of the letters, and Rand bristled. Jobs then accepted the commission without any further comment and took Rand's suggestion of renaming the company from Next to NeXT.

Dieter Rams, a German designer, is famous not only for his award-winning designs for consumer products (especially for Braun, where he was chief designer for thirty-four years) but also for his 'ten principles' embraced by Apple. One cannot overestimate Rams' importance in terms of his influence on Apple's design philosophy and product development. No study of Apple design is complete without carefully studying Rams' work.

Hartmut Esslinger of Frog Design was responsible for the look of Apple product in its early years. Jobs told him, 'I want our design not just to be the best in the personal computer industry but to be the best in the world.'[12]

Frog Design worked hand in hand with Jobs until he left the company after a power struggle with then-CEO John Sculley.

Esslinger's illuminating book, *Keep It Simple: The Early Design Years of Apple*, is required reading for anyone who is interested in the subject.

Jonathan ('Jony') Ive, currently the senior vice president of design at Apple Inc., is responsible for overseeing the Industrial Design Group. Ive's most famous designs for Apple include the MacBook Pro, iMac, MacBook Air, iPod, iPod Touch, iPhone, iPad, iPad Mini, and for the iPhone and iPads, the 'look' of iOS 7 (Operating System 7).

If there was one person at Apple whose sensibilities were precisely in tune with those of Jobs, surely that person is Jony Ive, whose work was influenced by Dieter Rams.

Ive is the subject of an unauthorised biography by Leander Kahney, *Jony Ive: The Genius Behind Apple's Greatest Products* (Portfolio/Penguin, 2013).

PRODUCTS IMPERFECT

Apple's handful of beautiful failures are dwarfed by the company's successes. But Apple learned from them, moved on and improved the product line. In other words, Apple iterated until it got things right.

Selected Books about Steve Jobs and Apple

Apple Confidential 2.0: The Definitive History of the World's Most Colorful Company, by Owen W. Linzmayer. No Starch Press, 2008. Trade paperback, 323 pages.

An excellent history of Apple with timelines and pertinent quotes from all the major players sprinkled throughout. Amply illustrated with photos, it has been expanded with 60 more pages than version 1.0. Newcomers will especially find it useful, especially those studying Apple's early years.

Gates: How Microsoft's Mogul Reinvented an Industry – and Made Himself the Richest Man in America, by Stephen Manes and Paul Andrews. Simon & Schuster/Touchstone, 1994. Trade paperback, 541 pages.

To appreciate and understand Steve Jobs, one must also understand Bill Gates and the turbulent times the two shared, for they are inextricably linked together.

This unauthorised biography on 'Trey' (his family nickname) is entertaining, authoritative and illuminating.

I, Steve: Steve Jobs in His Own Words, by George Beahm. Agate, 2011. Trade paperback, 160 pages.

The first quote book about Jobs, with a detailed timeline through 2011, it was a *New York Times* and an international bestseller.

iWoz: Computer Geek to Cult Icon, by Steve Wozniak with Gina Smith. Norton, 2006. Trade paperback, 313 pages.

Required reading for anyone who wants the inside scoop on what Jobs was like in the early years told from Woz's unique perspective. A gifted, self-taught engineer, he is universally respected in Silicon Valley.

Keep It Simple: The Early Design Years of Apple, by Hartmug Esslinger. Arnoldsche Art, 2013. Trade paperback, 283 pages.

Esslinger founded Frog Design, which worked with Jobs in the early years at Apple and at NeXT. Profusely illustrated with colour photos and concept drawings of various Apple products, the book is an insider's view to Apple's design philosophies.

More than a picture book, it's a textbook on how design is incorporated in Apple's consumer products. As Jobs liked to say, it's a rare peek inside the kimono.

Odyssey: Pepsi to Apple ... A Journey of Adventure, Ideas, and the Future, by John Sculley with John A. Byrne. Harper & Row, 1987. Trade hardback, 449 pages.

Remembered in the Apple community for his role in relieving Jobs of all operational responsibilities, John Sculley – a former president at PepsiCo and also former CEO and president of Apple – had an insider's view of what happened at Apple during that power struggle.

As Sculley makes very clear in his book, he didn't fire Jobs, as critics maintain; instead, in a power struggle between the two, Sculley asked the board to back him on his decision to relieve Jobs of all responsibilities as general manager of the Macintosh division while retaining the title of chairman of the board. The board did so, and Jobs left for several months on a sabbatical to Europe. Upon Jobs' return, he decided to resign as chairman of Apple and turn down the offer to remain as 'company visionary' to pursue a new start-up, NeXT.

Years later, in a lengthy interview published online, Sculley provided the most in-depth look at what happened back then, with the benefit of time's perspective. That interview can be accessed at:

http://www.cultofmac.com/63295/john-sculley-on-steve-jobs-the-full-interview-transcript/63295/

Return to the Little Kingdom: Steve Jobs, the Creation of Apple, and How It Changed the World, by Michael Moritz. Overlook Press, 2009. Trade hardback, 352 pages.

This edition updates the previous edition titled *The Little Kingdom: The Private Story of Apple Computer*, published in 1984. What makes this book unique is that Jobs initially authorised it and opened all the doors at Apple for Moritz – only to slam them shut after Moritz contributed to a *Time* magazine profile that enraged Jobs. 'Steve,' wrote Moritz in this book's prologue, 'made no secret of his anger and left a torrent of messages on the answering machine.'

After that encounter with the press, Jobs barred the door to all journalists wanting to write about Apple until he agreed to share his life's stories with Walter Isaacson, whom he explicitly trusted.

This book essentially covers Apple up to the time of the Mac's release in 1984, and does so in a thorough and entertaining manner – especially the early years. It also has an excellent index but suffers from a lack of photos. Even so, the book is indispensable reading, and belongs on the shelf of any Apple fan.

Steve Jobs, by Walter Isaacson. Simon & Schuster. Published in 2011 in hardback; the 2013 trade paperback added a much-needed epilogue for closure, providing details of Jobs' death and memorial services.

Though its length (631 pages) may intimidate some readers, this authorised biography is the one against which all other books on Steve Jobs must be measured. Jobs approached Isaacson, who had written major biographies on Albert Einstein, Benjamin Franklin and Henry Kissinger, to write his biography in the summer of 2004.

The detection of a tumour in Jobs' pancreas a year earlier was the catalyst for Steve Jobs and his wife to urge Isaacson to write the book as soon as possible.

Isaacson got to work on the book in 2009, after Jobs took a second medical leave of absence.

Drawing on over forty interviews with Jobs and over a hundred with family, friends, business associates and peers, Isaacson – a former managing editor for *Time* magazine – gives a straightforward accounting of Jobs' life and times.

Isaacson had free rein – a rare instance in which Jobs didn't want any control over the project, except (as it turns out) the cover design. (Jobs hated the original design and title; it showed a photo of him at the core of an apple, and its original title was *I, Steve.*)

The resultant book is required reading for anyone with more than a casual interest in Steve Jobs, whose reputation as a business visionary is undisputed.

Isaacson didn't shy away from discussing Jobs' personal faults, which were part of his essential nature. He could be – to say the very least – a difficult person to deal with, personally and professionally. (Jobs freely admitted to Isaacson that living with him wasn't exactly a bowl of cherries.)

The book is available in several editions and multiple formats. Get the trade paperback edition because of the added epilogue.

To Infinity and Beyond! The Story of Pixar Animation Studios, by Karen Paik. Chronicle Books, 2007. Trade hardback, 303 pages.

Sumptuously illustrated in full colour, elegantly designed and beautifully printed, this coffee-table book, though somewhat outdated, is simply delightful and enchanting. The colour reproduction, with spot varnish highlights, makes the artwork pop off the page.

Covering the company's backstory and then each film in chronological order up to *Cars*, this book is indispensable reading for anyone who wants the inside story of Pixar. (A complementary text, written by an outsider, *The Pixar Touch: The Making of a Company*, by David A. Pierce, is also recommended.)

OTHER BOOKS OF INTEREST

The Last Lecture, by Randy Pausch with Jeffrey Zaslow. Hyperion, 2008. Trade hardback, 206 pages.

Sadly, both Pausch and Zaslow are gone. Pausch had cancer of the liver, which killed him months after the initial diagnosis, and Zazlow ironically died in a car accident on the way back from a bookstore where he was signing *The Last Lecture*.

In most cases, the print version of a book and its e-book version are disappointingly identical, when in fact the e-book should be an enhanced version with numerous still photos in colour, audio and video. Happily, this e-book version, available from Apple's iBook store, takes advantage of the medium in full measure and is the edition of choice.

Much of what Pausch said recalls what Jobs said in various interviews over the years and specifically what Jobs said to Stanford graduates.

It's a small world, after all.

An Open Life: Joseph Campbell in Conversation with Michael Toms, selected and edited by John M. Maher and Dennie Briggs. Harper & Row/Perennial Library, 1990. Trade paperback, 137 pages.

An extended conversation between Campbell and Toms, this is an accessible introduction to mythologist Joseph Campbell, whose lifelong exploration of the nature of myth encompassed all the world's religions and cultures to find connective tissue. Thought-provoking and illuminating, the book ranges far and wide. (The source material is radio interviews originally broadcast on New Dimensions Radio between 1975 to 1987.)

The Quotable Walt Disney, compiled by Dave Smith. Disney Editions, 2001. Trade paperback, 263 pages.

Dave Smith, who was Disney's chief archivist/historian for forty years, brings together an excellent selection of quotations organised thematically, illustrated with photos and artwork.

Both Walt Disney and Steve Jobs were creative geniuses who thought so uncannily alike that it was no surprise their companies eventually merged. Both were visionaries, both were highly creative and imaginative, and both believed in the importance of the customer experience.

Jobs, who was only eleven years old when Disney died, would have recognised much of himself in *The Quotable Walt Disney*, because so many of the quotes could just as easily have been said by him.

Notes

STEVE JOBS' THREE STORIES

1. The Visible Measures Blog, 23 May 2013. No reliable estimates are available of how many people read the transcript, but it likely numbered in the millions; beyond its original posting, there were countless repostings, links and reprints on personal and business websites worldwide. Mallory Russell, 'Steve Jobs Tops the 10 Most Viewed Graduation Speeches', Visible Measures blog, web page, 23 May 2013, http://www.visiblemeasures.com/2013/05/23/steve-jobs-tops-the-10-most-viewed-graduation-speeches/.
2. Apple's Bud Tribble explains, 'The best way to describe the situation is a term from *Star Trek*. Steve has a reality distortion field ... In his presence, reality is malleable. He can convince anyone of practically anything. It wears off when he's not around, but it makes it hard to have realistic schedules.' Andy Hertzfeld, 'Reality Distortion Field', folklore.org, website http://www.folklore.org/StoryView.py?story=Reality_Distortion_Field.txt.
3. Pausch, who died of pancreatic cancer in 2008, delivered an address titled 'The Last Lecture' at Carnegie Mellon University in 2007. It is published in a book of that title by Pausch and Jeffrey Zaslow (Hyperion, 2008).
4. Apple co-founder Steve Wozniak delivered two commencement addresses.

5. Steve Jobs, 'Our DNA Hasn't Changed,' by CNNMoney, 21 February 2005, http://money.cnn.com/magazines/fortune/fortune_archive/2005/02/21/8251766/index.htm.
6. Staff written, 30th anniversary Apple ad celebrating the Macintosh, 24 January 1984, http://www.apple.com. Supplementary material at http://www.apple.com/30-years/.
7. Dave Smith, compiler, *Walt Disney: Famous Quotes* (Walt Disney Attractions Merchandise, 1994), 84.

CHAPTER 1

1. Joanne Schieble remarried and took the surname Simpson.
2. Stanford University web page, 'History of Stanford: The Rise of Silicon Valley', http://www.stanford.edu/about/history/history_ch3.html.
3. Hewlett-Packard web page, 'Quotes and Anecdotes about Bill Hewlett: On Bill's Generosity', http://www.hp.com/retiree/history/founders/hewlett/quotes.html.
4. Quoted in Walter Isaacson, *Steve Jobs* (Simon & Schuster, 2011), 40.
5. The annual tuition at Reed College in 1972 was $4,000.
6. Reed College web page, 'Facilities Services: History & Description', https://www.reed.edu/facilities_services/history.html.
7. Quoted in Isaacson, *Steve Jobs*, 40.
8. Jeremy Kahn, 'Is Harvard Worth It?' CNNMoney web page, 1 May 2000, http://money.cnn.com/magazines/fortune/fortune_archive/2000/05/01/278924/.
9. Other famous college dropouts include Microsoft's Bill Gates and Facebook's Mark Zuckerberg, both from Harvard.

CHAPTER 2

1. Quoted in Jeff Goodell, 'The Steve Jobs Nobody Knew', *Rolling Stone*, 1 November 2011, 38.
2. Bruce J. Klein, 'This Wonderful Lengthening of Lifespan', Fight Aging! web page, 17 January 2003, https://www.fightaging.org/archives/2003/01/this-wonderful-lengthening-of-lifespan.php.

3. David Sheff, 'Interview: Steven Jobs', *Playboy* (February 1985), 49.
4. Matt Lynley, 'Steve Jobs Was Working on the Next Apple Product the Day before He Died', *Business Insider* web page, 19 October 2011, http://www.businessinsider.com/steve-jobs-was-working-on-the-next-product-the-day-before-he-died-2011-10.
5. Brian Hiatt, 'Exclusive Q&A: Bono on Steve Jobs' Rock and Roll Spirit', rollingstone.com, 7 October 2011, http://www.rollingstone.com/music/news/exclusive-bono-on-steve-jobs-rock-and-roll-spirit-20111007.
6. *The Meditations of Marcus Aurelius Antoninus*, translated by Henry McCorman (Longman, Brown, Green, and Longmans, 1844), 51.

CHAPTER 3

1. Nobuyuki Hayashi, 'The Tales of Steve Jobs & Japan #03: Yukio Shakunaga, Steve Jobs' Favorite Porcelain Artist', Nobi.com web page, 11 February 2014, http://nobi.com/en/Steve%20Jobs%20and%20Japan/entry-1213.html.
2. Leander Kahney, 'John Sculley on Steve Jobs, the Full Interview Transcript', Cult of Mac web page, 14 October 2010, http://www.cultofmac.com/63295/john-sculley-on-steve-jobs-the-full-interview-transcript/.
3. Ibid.
4. Akio Morita, with Edwin M. Reingold and Mitsuko Shinomura, *Made in Japan* (E. P. Dutton, 1986), 207.
5. Ibid., 169–170.
6. Ibid., 206–207.
7. Brian Ashcraft, 'Apple Customers Escape Japanese Typhoon in Apple Store', Kotaku web page, 16 September 2013, http://kotaku.com/apple-customers-escape-japanese-typhoon-in-apple-store-1323652167.
8. Ibid.
9. *Made in Japan*, 210.
10. Ibid., 278.
11. Twitter feed, Tim Cook, 'Remembering Steve on his birthday', at 10.07 a.m., on 24 February 2014.
12. *Made in Japan*, 167.

CHAPTER 4

1. Jeffrey S. Young, *Steve Jobs: The Journey Is the Reward* (Scott, Foresman, 1988), 117.
2. Steve Wozniak quoted in Owen W. Linzmayer's *Apple Confidential 2.0* (No Starch Press, 2008), 13.
3. Andy Hertzfeld, *Revolution in the Valley* (O'Reilly Media Inc., 2005), 277.
4. Dave Smith, *Walt Disney: Famous Quotes* (Walt Disney Attractions Merchandise, 1994), 84.
5. Robert Cringely, *Steve Jobs: The Lost Interview* [recorded in 1995], DVD (Magnolia Pictures, 2012).
6. Hertzfeld, *Revolution in the Valley*, xv.
7. Ibid., 68.
8. Ibid.
9. Ibid., 277, 279.
10. Ibid.

CHAPTER 5

1. The partnership agreement, signed on 1 April 1976, included Ron Wayne, who had a 10 per cent share. But only eleven days after signing, he withdrew from the company, and is a minor footnote in Apple's history. Because of the brevity of his stay, he is typically not discussed as a co-founder.
2. This is an inside joke. In computing and telecommunications, a byte is an eight-bit unit of digital information.
3. Owen W. Linzmayer, *Apple Confidential 2.0* (No Starch Press, 2008), 7.
4. Apple I ad, *Interface Age* (July 1976).
5. Owen W. Linzmayer, *Apple Confidential 2.0* (No Starch Press, 2008), 7.
6. Ibid., 8.
7. Jason Green, 'Jobs House Added as "Historic Resource"', *San Jose Mercury News*, 28 October 2013, http://www.mercurynews.com/my-town/ci_24407428/jobs-house-cleared-apos-historic-resource.
8. Quoted in Susanna Kim, '10 Things You Didn't Know about Apple and Its Employees', 6 June 2013, ABC News web page, http://abcnews.go.com/Business/top-10-interesting-facts-apples-report-headquarters/story?id=19330088.

9. Kyle VanHemert, 'Look Inside Apple's Spaceship Headquarters with 24 All-New Renderings', *Wired*, 11 November 2013, http://www.wired.com/design/2013/11/a-glimpse-into-apples-crazy-new-spaceship-headquarters/.

CHAPTER 6

1. Steve Jobs, '"You've got to find what you love", Jobs says', news.stanford.edu, http://news.stanford.edu/news/2005/june15/jobs-061505.html.

CHAPTER 7

1. John M. Maher and Dennie Briggs, eds., *An Open Life: Joseph Campbell in Conversation with Michael Toms* (HarperCollins, 1990), 107.
2. Quoted in Walter Isaacson, *Steve Jobs* (Simon & Schuster, 2011), 16.
3. Steve Wozniak with Gina Smith, *iWoz* (W.W. Norton, 2006), 88.
4. Ibid., 119.
5. Quoted from Woz.org, Steve Wozniak's official website, http://www.woz.org/category/tags/apple-i.
6. Dave Smith, compiler, *Walt Disney: Famous Quotes* (Walt Disney Attractions Merchandise, 1994), 28.
7. Quoted in Robert Cringely, *Steve Jobs: The Lost Interview* [recorded in 1995], DVD (Magnolia Pictures, 2012).
8. Maher and Briggs, eds., *An Open Life*, 66.
9. Chenda Ngak, 'Steve Jobs remembered in emotional Apple video', cbsnews.com, http://www.cbsnews.com/news/steve-jobs-remembered-in-emotional-apple-video/.
10. Quoted in Cringely, *Steve Jobs: The Lost Interview*.
11. Arthur Schopenhauer, *The World as Will and Representation*, Vol II (Dover, 1958), 37.
12. 'i' for internet.
13. Quoted in Karen Paik, *To Infinity and Beyond!* (Chronicle Books, 2007), 47.
14. Quoted in Christopher John Farley, 'Pixar's John Lasseter on the Death of Steve Jobs', *Wall Street Journal*, 5 October 2011, http://blogs.wsj.com/speakeasy/2011/10/05/pixars-john-lasseter-on-the-death-of-steve-jobs/.

15. Alvy Ray Smith, who was, along with Ed Catmull, the management of Pixar, explains that Steve Jobs didn't buy Pixar from Lucasfilm. See his web page at: http://alvyray.com/Pixar/PixarMyth1.htm.
16. Quoted in Paik, *To Infinity and Beyond!*, 63.
17. Quoted in ibid.
18. Ina Fried and John Borland, 'Disney buys Pixar', 24 January, 2006, http://news.cnet.com/disney-buys-pixar/2100-1026_3-6030607.html.
19. Ibid.

CHAPTER 8

1. Steve Wozniak, *iWoz* (W.W. Norton & Company, 2006), 158.
2. Ibid., 178.
3. David Sheff, 'Steven Jobs: Interview', *Playboy* (February 1985), 58, 70.
4. Andy Hertzfeld, *Revolution in the Valley* (O'Reilly Media, 2005).
5. Quoted in ibid.
6. Apple public event debuting Macintosh in 1984, youtube.com, http://youtube.com/watch?v=lSiQA6KKyJo.
7. Quoted in Karen Paik, *To Infinity and Beyond!* (Chronicle Books, 2007).
8. Ibid., 90.
9. Ibid.
10. Diane Walker, *The Bigger Picture* (National Geographic, 2007), 60.

CHAPTER 9

1. Robert Cringely, *Steve Jobs: The Lost Interview* [recorded in 1995], DVD (Magnolia Pictures, 2012).
2. David Sheff, 'Interview: Steven Jobs', *Playboy* (February 1985), 49.
3. John Sculley with John A. Byrne, *Odyssey* (Harper & Row, 1987), 60.
4. Ibid., 77.
5. Ibid., 106.
6. Ibid., 119.
7. Ibid., 198.
8. Ibid., 85.
9. Danny Goodman, 'Interview: John Sculley', *Playboy* (September 1987), 53.
10. Sculley, *Odyssey*, 252.

11. Ibid., 52.
12. Steve Wozniak, *iWoz* (W.W. Norton & Company, 2006), 290.
13. Apple Computer press release, 'Apple Computer Plans to Streamline Operations and Increase Efficiency During Current Industry Pause', 31 May 1985.
14. Leander Kahney, 'John Sculley on Steve Jobs, The Full Interview Transcript', Cult of Mac website, 14 October 2010, http://www.cultofmac.com/63295/john-sculley-on-steve-jobs-the-full-interview-transcript/.

CHAPTER 10

1. Danny Goodman, 'Interview: John Sculley', *Playboy* (September, 1987), 53.
2. David Sheff, 'Interview: Steven Jobs', *Playboy* (February 1985), 182.
3. From William Wordsworth's poem, 'The Prelude', upon viewing a statue of Newton at Trinity College in Cambridge, England.

CHAPTER 11

1. David Sheff, 'Interview: Steven Jobs', *Playboy* (February 1985), 182.
2. After Paul Rand designed the company logo, NeXT, Jobs decided to change the company's name accordingly.
3. Walter Isaacson, *Steve Jobs* (Simon & Schuster, 2011), 235.
4. Neil McAllister, 'Steve Ballmer: Thanks to me, Microsoft screwed up a decade in phones', theregister.co.uk, 4 March 2014, http://www.theregister.co.uk/2014/03/04/microsoft_steve_ballmer_oxford/.
5. Diana Walker, *The Bigger Picture: Thirty Years of Portraits* (National Geographic, 2007), 60.
6. Ibid.
7. Karen Paik, *To Infinity and Beyond!* (Chronicle Books, 2007), 63.
8. Up to and including *Monsters, Inc.* (2013), see http://boxofficemojo.com/franchises/chart/?id=pixar.htm.

CHAPTER 12

1. John Sculley with John A. Byrne, *Odyssey* (Harper & Row, 1987), 69.
2. 'An Apple Fellow is a person who has been designated as such by Apple Inc. in recognition of his or her extraordinary technical or leadership

contributions to personal computing. Each Apple Fellow acts as a leader and visionary, guiding the company in their particular area of expertise. The Apple Fellowship has been awarded so far to very few individuals including Bill Atkinson, Don Norman, Alan Kay, Guy Kawasaki, Gursharan Sidhu, Gary Starkweather, and Steve Wozniak.' See 'Corporate Culture' in 'Apple Inc.', Wikipedia, http://en.wikipedia.org/wiki/Apple_Inc.

3. Owen Linzmayer, *Apple Confidential 2.0* (No Starch Press, 2008), 78.
4. Ibid., 43.
5. Ibid., 299.
6. Ibid.

CHAPTER 14

1. Mona Simpson, 'A Sister's Eulogy for Steve Jobs', *The New York Times*, 30 October 2011.
2. 'Steve Jobs Sings a New Tune', Stanford Graduate School of Business website, 29 May 2003, http://public2-prod.gsb.stanford.edu/news/headlines/vftt_jobs.shtml.
3. Ed Smith quoted in David A. Price, *The Pixar Touch: The Making of a Company* (Vintage Books, 2009), 114.
4. John Markoff, 'Apple's Visionary Redefined Digital Age', *The New York Times*, 5 October 2011.
5. Simpson, 'A Sister's Eulogy'.
6. 'Steve Jobs: Family Photo Album', Interview with Walter Isaacson, cbs.news.com, 15 July 2012, http://www.cbsnews.com/news/steve-jobs-family-photo-album/.
7. Quoted in Walter Isaacson, *Steve Jobs* (Simon & Schuster, 2011), 530.
8. Joseph Campbell with Bill Moyers, *The Power of Myth* (Doubleday, 1988), 250.

CHAPTER 15

1. Daniel Terdiman, 'John Sculley Spills the Beans on Firing Steve Jobs', CNET, 9 September 2013, http://news.cnet.com/8301-13579_3-57602004-37/john-sculley-spills-the-beans-on-firing-steve-jobs/.
2. Gil Amelio and William L. Simon, *On the Firing Line* (HarperBusiness, 1998), 271.

3. Brent Schlender and Wilton Woods, 'Something's Rotten in Cupertino …', money.cnn.com, 3 March 1997, http://money.cnn.com/magazines/fortune/fortune_archive/1997/03/03/222710/.
4. Robert Cringely, *Steve Jobs: The Lost Interview* [recorded in 1995], DVD (Magnolia Pictures, 2012).
5. Ibid.
6. Quoted in Brad Stone, 'Steve Jobs: The Return, 1977–2011', *Businessweek*, 6 October 2011.
7. Andy Hertzfeld, '90 Hours a Week and Loving It!' (October 1983), http://www.folklore.org/StoryView.py?story=90_Hours_A_Week_And_Loving_It.txt.
8. Lev Grossman and Harry McCracken, 'The Inventory of the Future', *Time*, 17 October 2011, http://content.time.com/time/magazine/article/0,9171,2096294,00.html.
9. This was used in early Apple Computer ads.
10. Apple Press Info, 'Apple Presents iPod', 23 October 2001, http://www.apple.com/pr/library/2001/10/23Apple-Presents-iPod.html.
11. Ibid.
12. Quoted in Microsoft News Center, 'Welcome to the Social', https://www.microsoft.com/en-us/news/features/2006/nov06/11-13zune.aspx.
13. Nick Wingfield, 'R.I.P. Zune', *The New York Times*, 4 June 2012, http://bits.blogs.nytimes.com/2012/06/04/r-i-p-zune/.
14. Matt Warman, 'iPod Inventor Tony Fadell on Apple, Steve Jobs and Nest', *The Telegraph*, 29 November 2012, http://www.telegraph.co.uk/technology/news/9708168/iPod-inventor-Tony-Fadell-on-Apple Steve-Jobs-and-Nest.html.

CHAPTER 16

1. David Sheff, 'Interview: Steven Jobs', *Playboy* (February 1985), 58.
2. Andy Reinhardt, 'Steve Jobs: First, Let's Kill All the Clones', *BusinessWeek* archives, 15 September 1997, http://www.businessweek.com/1997/37/b3544085.htm.
3. Quoted in Karen Paik, *To Infinity and Beyond!* (Chronicle Books, 2007), 147.
4. Quoted in ibid., 156.
5. Quoted in ibid., 157.

6. Brad Gibson, 'Jobs Slams Retail Buying; Defends Apple Stores', macworld.com, 15 January 2001, http://www.macworld.com/article/1021696/jobs.html.
7. Sculley, taking a page from his successful 'Pepsi Challenge' in which the consumer was offered a taste test between Coke and Pepsi, tried to repeat history with a 'take a Mac home to test drive' but only once: It proved to be a gimmicky failure. As *Apple Confidential 2.0* explained on page 55, 'About 200,000 people participated in the program, eagerly lugging brand-new Macs home for a day … Apple … discovered the 'Test Drive' program was more like a train wreck … Apple had wagered that program participants would become so enamoured of their new toys that they'd decide to buy them outright instead of return them after 24 hours. Apple lost that bet as the vast majority of the loaner Macs were returned slightly worse for wear.'
8. Apple Press Info, 'Apple to Open 25 Retail Stores in 2001', 15 May 2001, https://www.apple.com/pr/library/2001/05/15Apple-to-Open-25-Retail-Stores-in-2001.html.
9. Quoted in Cliff Edwards, 'Commentary: Sorry, Steve: Here's Why Apple Stores Won't Work', Bloomberg Businessweek, 20 May 2001, http://www.businessweek.com/stories/2001-05-20/commentary-sorry-steve-heres-why-apple-stores-wont-work.

CHAPTER 17

1. Blog of Lisa Brennan-Jobs: Essays. Published in *Vogue* (February 2008), 'Tuscan Holiday', 4 September 2009, http://www.lisabrennanjobs.net/2009/09/tuscan-holiday.html.
2. Quoted in Walter Isaacson, *Steve Jobs* (Simon & Schuster, 2011), 280.
3. John Paczkowski, 'Steve Jobs, in His Own Words', 5 October 2011, http://allthingsd.com/20111005/steve-jobs-in-his-own-words/.
4. Mona Simpson, 'A Sister's Eulogy for Steve Jobs', *The New York Times*, 30 October 2011.
5. Jill Smolowe, 'Steve Jobs 1955–2011', *People*, 24 October 2011, 72.
6. Ibid.
7. *Daily Mail* Reporter, 'Still Holding on to His Son's Legacy: Steve Jobs' Biological Father Clings to His iPhone as He Reveals His Grief', MailOnline, 11 October 2011, http://www.dailymail.co.uk/news

/article-2047588/Steve-Jobs-dead-Father-Abdulfattah-John-Jandali-son-met.html.

8. Daniel Bates, '"I live in hope he will reach out to me before it's too late": Steve Jobs' biological father speaks of yearning to meet his son', dailymail.co.uk, http://www.dailymail.co.uk/news/article-2031575/Steve-Jobs-biological-father-speaks-yearning-meet-son.html.
9. Daily Mail Reporter, 'Still holding on to his son's legacy: Steve Jobs' biological father clings to his iPhone as he reveals his grief', 11 October 2011, http://www.dailymail.co.uk/news/article-2047588/Steve-Jobs-dead-Father-Abdulfattah-John-Jandali-son-met.html.
10. Loreena McKennitt, 'News & Views: The View from Here', *Loreena's Holiday Reflections* 1, no. 7, quinlanroad.com, 31 December 2013, http://www.quinlanroad.com/newsandviews/theviewfromhere.asp.

CHAPTER 18

1. David Sheff, 'Interview: Steven Jobs', *Playboy* (February 1985), 182.
2. Ibid.

CHAPTER 19

1. Chrisann Brennan, *The Bite in the Apple: A Memoir of My Life with Steve Jobs* (St. Martin's Press, 2014), Kindle Edition.
2. Daniel Morrow, 'Steve Jobs Interview: One-on-One in 1995', *Computerworld* web page, 6 October 2011, http://www.computerworld.com/s/article/9220609/Steve_Jobs_interview_One_on_one_in_1995?taxonomyId=214&pageNumber=10.
3. Joe Nocera, 'Apple's Culture of Secrecy', *The New York Times*, 26 July 2008, http://www.nytimes.com/2008/07/26/business/26nocera.html?sq=&st=nyt&scp=170&pagewanted=all&_r=0.
4. Walter Isaacson, *Steve Jobs* (Simon & Schuster, 2011), 51.

CHAPTER 20

1. Sharon Betley, 'Jobs's Unorthodox Treatment', thedailybeast.com, 5 October 2011, http://www.thedailybeast.com/articles/2011/10/05/steve-jobs-dies-his-unorthodox-treatment-for-neuroendocrine-cancer.html.

CHAPTER 21

1. Stewart Brand, 'We Are as Gods', *Whole Earth Catalog* (Fall 1968), 3.
2. Stewart Brand quoted by J. Baldwin, *Ecological Design: Inventing the Future* Amazon Digital Services, Inc. [documentary], 1994.
3. David Sheff, 'Interview: Steven Jobs', *Playboy* (February 1985), 52.
4. Video interview with Steve Jobs, *Memory & Imagination: New Pathways to the Library of Congress*, DVD, directed by Julian Krainin and Michael R. Lawrence (Krainin Productions, 1990).
5. Quoted in Rama Dev Jager and Rafael Ortiz, *In the Company of Giants: Candid Conversations with the Visionaries of the Digital World* (McGraw-Hill, 1997), 24–25.
6. Dave Smith, compiler, *The Quotable Walt Disney* (Disney Editions, 2001), 41.

CHAPTER 22

1. Stewart Brand, quoted in Carole Cadwalladr, 'Stewart Brand's Whole Earth Catalog, the Book that Changed the World', theguardian.com, 4 May 2013, http://www.theguardian.com/books/2013/may/05/stewart-brand-whole-earth-catalog.
2. Robert Cringely, *Steve Jobs: The Lost Interview* [recorded in 1995], DVD (Magnolia Pictures, 2012).
3. Mike Cassidy, 'Cassidy on Nolan Bushnell: "Steve Was Difficult", Says Man Who First Hired Steve Jobs', *San Jose Mercury News*, 28 March 2013, http://www.mercurynews.com/ci_22890892/cassidy-steve-jobs-hire-nolan-bushnell-book-atari.
4. Nolan Bushnell with Gene Stone, *Finding the Next Steve Jobs* (Simon & Schuster, 2013), 225.
5. Shashank Chouhan, 'Indian Visit Gave a Vision to Steve Jobs', indiatoday.in, 13 October 2011, http://indiatoday.intoday.in/story/india-visit-gave-a-vision-to-steve-jobs/1/154785.html.
6. Brett T. Robinson, *Appletopia: Media Technology and the Religious Imagination of Steve Jobs* (Baylor University Press, 2013), 86.
7. Definition of 'freethinker', *The American Heritage Dictionary of the English Language*, fourth edition (Houghton Mifflin Company, 2000), 701.

ONE MORE THING … LETTING GO

1. When forced from Apple Computer, he founded NeXT, which he ran for eleven years.
2. Rachel Metz, Associated Press, 'Apple co-founder Wozniak says he'll miss Jobs', USA TODAY|Tech, 5 October 2011, web page, http://usatoday30.usatoday.com/tech/news/story/2011-10-06/wozniak-reacts-jobs-death/50676712/1.
3. Apple Press Info, email to all Apple employees, 5 October 2011, https://www.apple.com/pr/library/2011/10/05Apple-Media-Advisory.html.
4. John Lasseter and Ed Catmull, 5 October 2011, web page, www.pixar.com.
5. Kori Schulman, The White House Blog, 'President Obama on the Passing of Steve Jobs: "He changed the way each of us sees the world"', 5 October 2011, web page, whitehouse.gov, http://www.whitehouse.gov/blog/2011/10/05/president-obama-passing-steve-jobs-he-changed-way-each-us-sees-world.
6. Nick Eaton, 'Bill Gates on death of Steve Jobs: "I will miss Steve immensely"', 5 October 2011, web page, blog.seattlepi.com, http://blog.seattlepi.com/microsoft/2011/10/05/bill-gates-on-death-of-steve-jobs-i-will-miss-steve-immensely/.
7. Staff written, 'Tributes Pour In for Steve Jobs', *Rolling Stone*, 6 October 2011, web page, http://www.rollingstone.com/culture/news/tributes-pour-in-for-steve-jobs-20111006.

CONNECTING THE DOTS

1. Quoted in John Markoff, 'The Passion of Steve Jobs', *The New York Times*, 15 January 2008.
2. David Sheff, 'Interview: Steven Jobs', *Playboy* (February 1985), 184.
3. Nolan Bushness with Gene Stone, *Finding the Next Steve Jobs* (Simon & Schuster, 2013), 8.
4. Steve Wozniak with Gina Smith, *iWoz* (Norton, 2006), 92.
5. Apple Press Info, 'The Beatles Now on iTunes', 16 November 2010.
6. Hartmut Esslinger, *Keep It Simple* (Arnoldsche Art, 2013), 279.
7. Press release, 'Masterworks by Tiffany Studios: A Sutton Place Collection', 4 June 2013, http://www.christies.com/presscenter/pdf/2013/release_3419.pdf.

8. Jim Davis, 'Apple's Jobs gets jet, shares in bonus', CNET News, 19 January 2000, http://news.cnet.com/2100-1040-235835.html.
9. Betsy Morris, 'Steve Jobs, Obsession, and Those Whales', *Wired*, 7 October 2011, http://www.wired.com/business/2011/10/column-jobs-obsession-whales/.
10. Andy Hertzfeld, 'Mister Macintosh' (February 1982). folklore.org, http://www.folklore.org/StoryView.py?project=Macintosh&story=Mister_Macintosh.txt&showcomments=1.
11. 'NeXT logo by Paul Rand', logodesignlove.com, 29 March 2010, http://www.logodesignlove.com/next-logo-paul-rand.
12. Esslinger, *Keep It Simple*, 11.

JAICO PUBLISHING HOUSE

Elevate Your Life. Transform Your World.

ESTABLISHED IN 1946, Jaico Publishing House is home to world-transforming authors such as Robin Sharma, Sadhguru, Osho, the Dalai Lama, Deepak Chopra, Eknath Easwaran, Paramhansa Yogananda, Devdutt Pattanaik, Radhakrishnan Pillai, Morgan Housel, Napoleon Hill, John Maxwell, Brian Tracy and Stephen Hawking.

Our late founder Mr. Jaman Shah first established Jaico as a book distribution company. Sensing that independence was around the corner, he aptly named his company Jaico ('Jai' means victory in Hindi). In order to service the significant demand for affordable books in a developing nation, Mr. Shah initiated Jaico's own publications. Jaico was India's first publisher of paperback books in the English language.

While self-help, religion and philosophy, mind, body and spirit, and business titles form the cornerstone of our non-fiction list, we publish an exciting range of current affairs, history, biography, art and architecture, travel, and popular science books as well. Our renewed focus on popular fiction is evident in our new titles by a host of fresh young talent from India and abroad.

Jaico's translations division publishes select best-selling titles in over 10 regional languages including Gujarati, Hindi, Kannada, Malayalam, Marathi, Tamil, and Telugu. These include titles from renowned national and international authors like Sudha Murthy, Gaur Gopal Das, Swami Mukundananda, Jay Shetty, Simon Sinek, Ankur Warikoo and Jeff Keller.

Boasting one of India's largest book distribution networks, Jaico has its headquarters in Mumbai, with branches in Ahmedabad, Bangalore, Chennai, Delhi, Hyderabad, and Kolkata. This network ensures that our books reach all parts of the country, both urban and rural.